THE DEATH OF
ALBERT JOHNSON
MAD TRAPPER of RAT RIVER

F.W. Anderson and Art Downs

Heritage
House

National Library of Canada Cataloguing in Publication

The death of Albert Johnson
Based on the previous eds. by Frank W. Anderson.

ISBN 1-894384-03-2

1. Johnson, Albert, d. 1932. 2. Police murders—Rat River Region (Yukon and N.W.T.)
3. Criminals—Rat River Region (Yukon and N.W.T.)—Biography. I. Anderson, Frank W.,
1919-   —Death of Albert Johnson.

FC4172.1.J6D42 2000   364.1'523'097191   C00-910117-9
F1060.9.J6D42 2000

First edition, 1968, reprinted six times; revised edition 1980, 1982, 1986, reprinted 1989, 1991;
First Heritage House edition, 2000, reprinted 2004.

Heritage House acknowledges the financial support for our publishing program from the Government of Canada through the Book Publishing Industry Development Program (BPIDP), Canada
Council for the Arts, and the British Columbia Arts Council.

HERITAGE HOUSE PUBLISHING COMPANY LTD.
Unit #108 – 17665 66A Ave., Surrey, BC V3S 2A7

Printed in Canada

BRITISH
COLUMBIA
ARTS COUNCIL
We acknowledge the support of the Province of British Columbia
through the British Columbia Arts Council

The Canada Council | Le Conseil des Arts
for the Arts | du Canada

The cover
This painting by John Moutray shows the *Bellanca*, piloted by Wop May, skimming over the
Eagle River as the pursuit of Albert Johnson reached its climax.
John's subjects include wildlife, dogs, and aircraft. The latter is his favourite, which is not
surprising since John served in the RAF and the RCAF during World War II, winning both the
DFM and DFC. A former art director of Evergreen Press, John retired in Langley, B.C.

Photo credits
City of Edmonton Archives, 44, 82; Department of Energy, Mines and Resources, 58-59, 72-73;
Glenbow Archives, 1, 6-7, 28-29, 30, 32, 34-35, 37, 38, 46, 76-77, 83, 86-87, 88, 91; Wop May, 3,
40-41, 54-55, 60-61, 64-65, 67, 68-69; Public Archives Canada, 9, 12, 17, 90, 92; RCMP, 14-15,
17, 19, 21, 22-23, 25, 26, 44, 47, 50-51; Copyright Frank Slim, Joe Lindsay, Dick North, 4.

Acknowledgements
Appreciation is expressed to those who assisted in preparing this book: John Millen, Ladner, B.C.;
Staff Sergeant T.E.G. Shaw, RCMP, retired; Arthur Know and Elmer Scott, Calgary, Alberta;
Georgina Barrass and Margaret Howson, Glenbow Foundation, Calgary, Alberta; and personnel of
the RCMP Museum, Regina, Saskatchewan.

CONTENTS

Wop May's Bellanca aircraft, here being loaded with supplies from the Aklavik Hudson's Bay Company store, played a prominent role in the Albert Johnson manhunt.

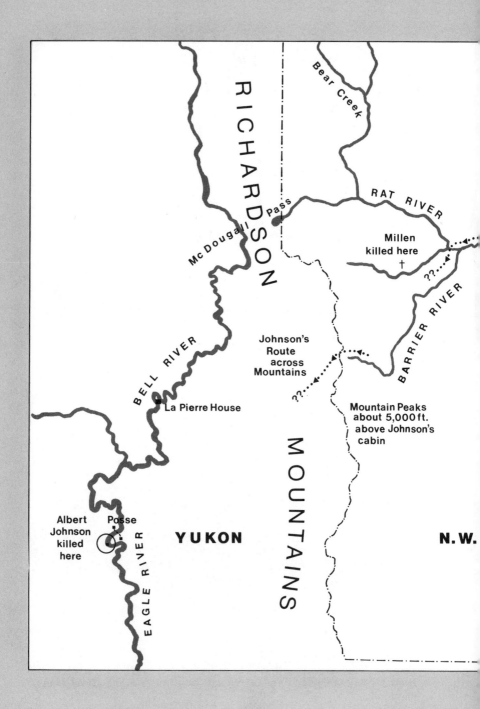

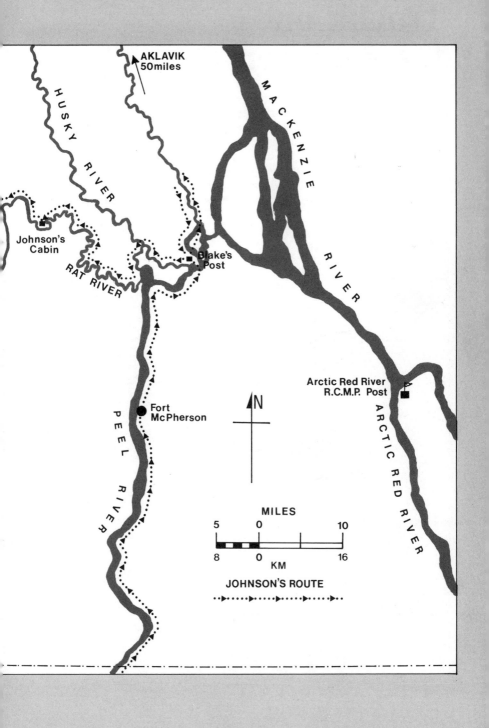

AKLAVIK
50miles

H U S K Y

R I V E R

Johnson's
Cabin

RAT RIVER

M A C K E N Z I E

R I V E R

Blake's
Post

P E E L

R I V E R

Fort
McPherson

Arctic Red River
R.C.M.P. Post

A R C T I C   R E D   R I V E R

N

MILES

5   0   10

8   0   16
KM

JOHNSON'S ROUTE

Trouble on the Rat River

Two kinds of patrols were carried out by Constable Edgar Millen and his two-man detachment of Royal Canadian Mounted Police at Arctic Red River, a tiny settlement just south of the Arctic Circle. The first were "routine" patrols whereby the detachment visited isolated cabins, delivered mail, discreetly checked on men who wanted to be left alone, and performed a hundred and one civil service duties throughout the region. The second were "special" patrols; that is, trips made for a specific reason such

The Rat River near the Arctic Ocean. In sub-zero cold during the winter of 1932 it made headlines across North America.

as a mercy mission, escort duty for a visiting dignitary, or investigation into a reported crime. An interesting aspect of the work was that the policemen were never certain until the patrol was completed if it was a routine or a special mission.

The patrol that set out on July 20, 1931, started as a routine one. It was destined to end in tragedy.

Constable Millen was born in Belfast, Ireland, in 1901. Prior to

emigrating with his parents to Canada, he had attended the tough Curragh Camp, a military school for boys where he acquired a lifelong distaste for routine, spit and polish. In spite of this aversion, however, he joined the Royal Canadian Mounted Police in 1920. After several postings to Regina, Winnipeg and Edmonton, he volunteered for northern duty and was sent to Aklavik, headquarters of the Western Arctic Sub-District, in June 1923. From then on most of his service was in the Northwest Territories, broken only by brief holidays with his family in Edmonton. One other diversion from the routine occurred after his superiors learned that he was the finest pastry cook in the northland. This talent did not go unused, especially when notable travellers such as the Governor-General visited Aklavik.

In the summer of 1931 on his return to Aklavik from a holiday in Edmonton, Millen was offered a Corporal's stripes and the post at Arctic Red River, a small base some 110 km (70 miles) south of Aklavik. Because of his dislike for paper work he declined but reckoned without the sardonic humor of his superiors. It wasn't long before Millen found himself in charge of the detachment, minus the stripes, but saddled with the paperwork.

One of Constable Millen's duties on his July patrol to Fort McPherson 80 km (50 miles) to the west of his small post was to check on a newcomer to the district. From a radio report out of Aklavik, Millen learned that a man named Albert Johnson had arrived at Fort McPherson on July 9, after rafting down the Peel River from the direction of Dawson. News of his arrival had been taken to Aklavik by Bishop Geddes. A routine order to investigate was issued by the Commanding Officer of the Western Arctic Sub-District, Inspector A.N. Eames.

The RCMP's interest in Johnson was not aroused by suspicious actions but reflected the force's concern for individuals moving into the north. The Depression of the thirties was worsening throughout Canada and men with a distaste for civilization and its breadlines constantly sought to escape into the northern wilderness. Because many arrived without money and were poorly equipped to survive in the harsh north, the police discouraged them from settling even briefly in the Arctic. This was Millen's purpose in seeking out Albert Johnson.

Millen reached Fort McPherson on July 21 and had no difficulty finding Johnson who was camped a short distance from the community. He was a man of about forty years, of medium height and weight, with receding brown hair and diffident blue eyes. A man without striking features, except for his arms which seemed longer than normal for a man of his height.

Millen received a cool reception and little information from the taciturn Johnson. Apparently he had spent the summer of 1930 on the Canadian prairies and entered the north via the Mackenzie River system, but he made no mention of where he had spent the previous winter. He told Millen he intended to go into the Rat River country some 30 km (20 miles) north and west of Fort McPherson as soon as he had replaced his outfit which he said he had lost.

There was little Millen could do, but he left Johnson with the warning that if he planned to trap in the Rat River district, he would have to obtain a licence from either Arctic Red River or Aklavik. Back at Fort McPherson, the Constable made a few enquiries. Although Johnson had only a meagre

8

The small outposts of Arctic Red River, above, and Fort McPherson in 1920. At Fort McPherson Johnson bought a shotgun, canoe and other supplies.

outfit he appeared to be well supplied with money, since he had purchased a 16-gauge single-barrel shotgun and a box of shells from the Northern Traders store, and was buying supplies from the Hudson's Bay post. In his dealings, however, he had been close-lipped about his past and immediate plans.

There the matter rested.

A week after his interview with Millen, Albert Johnson purchased a large canoe from a local Indian and left Fort McPherson on July 28, paddling leisurely down the Peel River, passing but not stopping at Arthur Blake's small trading post at the mouth of the Husky River. Four days later he returned up river, stroking skilfully against the current, and beached at the post. He told Blake he was looking for the Rat River turnoff but had missed the main branch. However, he was confident he could reach the Rat by travelling up a small creek behind the trading post and making a series of short portages.

Blake was doubtful. He knew the north, having served some six years with the Royal North West Mounted Police before taking his discharge and establishing his trading post. He voiced his concern and advised Johnson to return up the Peel and follow the south branch of the Husky to the Rat. But Johnson was confident of his own abilities and left that afternoon, paddling his heavily laden canoe up the creek towards the sparsely inhabited wilderness of the Rat River.

Although ex-policeman Blake didn't realize it, he had no reason to be concerned about Johnson's ability to survive in the wilderness. Albert Johnson was a resolute man of unusual strength and stamina, hardened to back-breaking work, loneliness and isolation. He also had fanatical confidence in his ability to handle any situation — alone, as subsequent events would prove. He now fought his way through the rugged country behind Blake's post, packing both load and heavy canoe over the rocky portages to the mouth of the Rat River.

A few miles above its mouth, the Rat River is joined by Driftwood Creek. At this junction are a series of rapids so dangerous that during the stampede to Klondike in 1898 many a canoe and outfit were destroyed and the gold miners dolefully dubbed the section "Destruction City." It was no deterrent to Johnson. He negotiated the treacherous stretch single-handed, and continued up the Rat River some 25 km (15 miles) from its confluence with the south branch of the Husky. Here on a wooded promontory bounded on three sides by the river, he built a cabin of a type common among trappers.

First he dug a hole about 3 ft. deep and approximately 8 by 12 feet. Around this excavation he built log walls 5 ft. high. Because few of the available trees were straight, there were large spaces in the walls and roof. These he plugged with dirt. The pole roof was sloped from 5 ft. high in the front to 4 ft. at the back and covered with 2 ft. of dirt.

On one side he inserted a small window and beside it a door only large enough for him to enter. The left wall of the cabin which faced an open clearing between the house and the river bank he protected against the wind by an additional wall. Heating and cooking facilities were provided by a light, tin-can type of stove.

Surveyors in the north struggle over a rapids with a canoe hewn from a cottonwood tree. Johnson fought up similar rapids by himself.

Much was subsequently written about the "fort-like" construction of Albert Johnson's cabin, and many inferred that it was built to withstand attack. It is more probable, however, that the design was dictated by the availability of material, the severity of Arctic winters, and the fact that he was working alone. Also, it seems probable that Johnson intended it to be a permanent structure, unlike many cabins in the Territories which were built for temporary summer use.

A cautious man, Johnson kept only a portion of his supplies in the cabin. Apparently guarding against the possibility of fire, he concealed the remainder a short distance away in a "stage cache" — a wooden platform suspended in the short, stubby trees.

Despite his retiring nature, the presence of Albert Johnson in the district drew no unusual attention from the Mounted Police. The north was a land of live and let live. If a man wanted to be alone, no one bothered him. It was a land where men threw up a cabin, used it for a time and then moved on — perhaps to better trapping or hunting grounds, perhaps impelled by restlessness. Except for the Indians who travelled in small groups, many men preferred distance between themselves and their nearest neighbor. Occasionally, continued exposure to months of snow, darkness and sub-zero weather brought on cases of mental illness. On these occasions, the police rescued the unfortunate victims from the consequences of their self-imposed isolation.

Typical of this independent breed was George Lux who at eighty-four lived alone in a cabin some 80 km (50 miles) from Aklavik as independent as

Aklavik, above in 1930, was the focal point of the search for Albert Johnson.

a crusty old porcupine. One winter he injured his eye while chopping wood. Too weak to attempt the winter journey alone, he suffered excruciating pain and was on the verge of committing suicide when an Indian found him and carried word to Aklavik. Constable R.G. McDowell, one of the fastest dog-team men in the area, made a mercy trip to bring the old-timer to hospital at Aklavik. Once cured, George Lux went back to his solitary cabin.

Johnson fitted into this pattern — except for one detail. While he wanted to be left alone, he made the mistake of interfering with others.

Towards the middle of December 1931, while following his trap lines, Johnson found that some Loucheux Indians from the Rat River district had set traps near his. He removed them, then slung them over the limb of a tree. When the Indians discovered that their traps had been removed they reported the incident to Constable Millen at Arctic Red River, even though it meant a mid-winter trek of over 110 km (70 miles).

On December 26, Constable Millen dispatched his entire force — Constables King and Bernard — to investigate the complaint and to ascertain whether Johnson had obtained the trapper's licence which Millen had advised him to get in July. It did not appear that he had done so from either Aklavik or Arctic Red River.

Constable King, a quiet, efficient young man from Montreal, left with Bernard and a dog team in the pitch black of early morning. It was bitterly cold. They reached Fort McPherson and spent the night comfortably, a warm contrast to the following night when they camped at the mouth of the Rat River in the open in 30-below temperature.

The next morning they arrived at Johnson's cabin just after dawn — about 10 a.m. at that time of year. Leaving the dog team on the frozen river, they climbed the steep bank to the clearing. A wisp of smoke from the chimney and a pair of crude snowshoes beside the squat door indicated that Johnson was in the cabin or close by.

King rapped on the door. There was no response. He continued to knock, announcing that he was a police officer and that he wanted to speak to the occupant. Still there was no reply. In a land where doors were never locked and where any traveller was welcome — at least for a while — Johnson's behavior was considered not only strange but hostile.

The two men spent nearly an hour trying to persuade Johnson to let them in, but he refused even to acknowledge their presence. Once, King noticed Johnson watching from the window. Johnson immediately dropped the curtain and acted as if they were nuisances and he a patient man waiting for them to leave.

Finally King gave up. He and Bernard returned to the sled to discuss the situation. Even allowing for the peculiarities brought on by isolation, they considered Johnson's conduct hinted at problems more serious than resentment of Indians trapping close to his lines, or lack of a trapper's licence. There was an arrogance, too, that suggested trouble. No matter how much a man desired to be left alone, there were certain courtesies traditionally extended to visitors.

As King had no way of communicating with Constable Millen at Arctic Red River, he decided to report to Inspector Eames at Headquarters in Aklavik some 130 km (80 miles) away.

A Rifle Shatters the Silence

Inspector Eames shared the concern of Constable King over Johnson's unfriendly behavior. From the meagre information gleaned by Constable Millen, he knew the newcomer was taciturn and independent to the point of rudeness. Johnson's last act of insolence, however, indicated that he was determined to maintain his independence of all men and authorities.

Eames issued King a search warrant and reinforced his party with the addition of Constable Robert McDowell, a veteran Arctic policeman, and Special Constable Lazarus Sittichiulis. The four policemen left Aklavik carrying rifles in addition to their side arms. After an over-night camp on

The .30-30 rifle with which Johnson killed Constable Millen and nearly killed Constable A.W. King, opposite, and Staff Sergeant H.F. Hersey.

the trail, they reached Johnson's cabin the next morning, the last day of the year.

Once again, a wisp of smoke and snowshoes beside the door indicated Johnson's presence. Leaving his companions on the frozen river below the steep bank, Constable King crossed the clearing and walked to the cabin. He rapped on the door. "Are you there, Mr. Johnson?"

A rifle bullet fired through the closed door was his answer. It hit King in the chest. Stunned by the impact, he slumped into the snow.

For a moment the three men waiting below the bank were mesmerized by the unprovoked and vicious attack. Then Constable McDowell, realizing King was exposed to a follow-up shot, snatched his Lee-Enfield from the sled and opened fire. He hoped to disable Johnson or at least distract his attention from the wounded constable lying outside the cabin door.

The diversion succeeded. Johnson aimed his rifle at McDowell and the two special constables. His first shot was wide but his second narrowly missed McDowell as he pumped bullets into the log walls. Meanwhile, King dragged himself round the end of the cabin. He managed to stand, then stagger towards the scanty clump of trees overlooking the river and slide down the embankment to safety.

McDowell, keeping out of sight of the cabin, reached King's side and saw that the policeman's condition was grave. He hastily threw most of the supplies off the toboggan and placed the wounded man on it. Then with Bernard and Sittichiulis bringing up the rear, McDowell headed for Aklavik and medical help.

In the dramatic race for his life across the frozen wastes of the northland, Constable King could have had no better man than McDowell. The previous year on the mail run from Aklavik to Baillie Island, McDowell had made incredible day marches of 80 to 100 km (50 to 65 miles) as a matter of routine. Now with an emergency on his hands, he drove himself, the dogs and the two Special Constables mercilessly. Fortunately King's wound was a clean one with little bleeding. The main danger stemmed from shock and the intense cold.

Even when darkness fell, he continued guiding the heavy toboggan carefully across the rough tundra and drifted snow. Sometimes Bernard and Sittichiulis had to run ahead, breaking trail for the laboring dogs; at other times they followed, straining to maintain McDowell's gruelling pace. They accomplished the 130-km (80-mile) trip — which normally took two days — in twenty hours, arriving at Aklavik Hospital in the early hours of January 1, 1932.

The wounded man was placed immediately under the care of the Assistant Surgeon whose examination revealed that the bullet had penetrated King's body in a straight line and passed within an inch of his heart. Had King not been bending over as he pounded on the cabin door, and had Johnson not fired from a position below ground level, the bullet would undoubtedly have ranged up through the constable's chest, killing him instantly.

Although Inspector Eames had equipped his first patrol-in-force with rifles, he had not expected armed resistance from Johnson. While at first the officers had suspected that Johnson was suffering mental illness, they

Inspector A.N. Eames was in charge of the hunt for Johnson. Below is the Royal Canadian Corps of Signals wireless station at Aklavik. The hunt for Johnson was the first in which radio was used for police work in Canada.

now felt otherwise. They had a growing conviction, supported by years of experience, that the trapper's actions sprang from an intense hatred of the police rather than depression brought on by isolation. The events of the next few weeks strengthened that belief. They were convinced that Johnson had had contact with the police and from that experience stemmed his bitter grudge. But whatever the cause of Johnson's behavior, it was the Inspector's job to bring him to justice. This duty was to prove more formidable than Eames or anyone else so far involved imagined. It also would have tragic consequences.

In the event that Johnson refused to surrender, Eames had two alternatives — surround the cabin and try to wait him out, or break in and drag him out. In either case the operation would require a large number of men, dogs and provisions. His command consisted of himself, a corporal, six regular constables and one special. The Arctic Red River police post had two constables and one special, but most of these men were required for regular duties.

If he sent a small posse, the result might be another rebuff from the entrenched trapper since from all reports the cabin was sturdily constructed and probably impervious to bullets. If he sent a large assault force, he would have difficulty supplying them and the dogs with provisions for the 130-km (80-mile) run. His problems intensified when on January 2, the temperature dropped to 40 below zero.

Eames finally decided to head a party of six men and forty-two dogs. He left Aklavik on January 4 with Constable McDowell, Special Constables Bernard and Sittichiulis, and three trappers, including lanky Knut Lang. Lang was a notable character in the North who had arrived at Aklavik in 1928, having worked his passage by cutting wood on a Mackenzie River steamer. Landing with only an axe and his gun, he soon carved himself a niche in the community and was known far and wide as a quick witted, generous giant. He was self-educated and after the Johnson affair, became an outspoken and often politically disturbing voice on the Northwest Territorial Council.

Inspector Eames had also radioed Constable Millen, instructing him to meet the posse at Arthur Blake's post on the Husky River. Another message went to the Hudson's Bay trader at Fort McPherson asking him to send Indian guide Charlie Rat to Blake's post.

Before reaching Blake's Post the following evening, Inspector Eames found himself plagued by the problem of supplies that was to hamper efforts to bring in Albert Johnson. The intense cold not only decreased the efficiency of his force to thirty per cent of normal but also depleted his provisions far quicker than anticipated. Only one day out of Aklavik the dog supplies had to be replenished.

The following morning, remembering that Johnson's cabin was solidly built, Eames had the foresight to add twenty pounds of dynamite from Blake's storehouse to his supplies.

As soon as Constable Millen — the only man who had seen Johnson face to face — and Charlie Rat arrived, Eames headed across country to the Rat River. He took the cross-country route since he felt that Johnson might expect them to travel up the Rat by the route taken by King on his two previous visits. The new route would also bypass a deep rugged canyon that had several places where a determined killer could cover the trail. While no one believed Johnson would try to ambush such a large party, Inspector Eames was taking no chances with a man who had shot without provocation or warning.

The detour should have followed an old trap line, but Charlie Rat either was uncertain of the route or still under the influence of too much New Year's celebrating at Fort McPherson. When the posse reached Rat River on January 7, they discovered that they were some 10 km (6 miles) above the cabin instead of behind it.

More time was lost, more provisions consumed, and more strength drained as the party returned to the first camp. With the temperature still hovering around 40 below zero, they spent the night only a few miles from Johnson's cabin.

Since supplies were running low and Inspector Eames had lost faith in Charlie Rat's sense of direction, he broke camp at daybreak and decided to move directly up river to the cabin. A telltale plume of smoke rose from the tin pipe — Johnson was still there.

Using the high river bank for cover, the Inspector moved to within 20 m (65 ft.) of the menacingly quiet cabin and ordered Johnson to come out. There was no reply. Eames repeated his command, adding that they were determined to arrest him and that resistance was useless.

Again Eames' command was met with silence from the squat, snow-covered cabin. There were no belligerent shouts or cries of defiance which

Constable R.G. McDowell. His skill as a dog musher saved Constable King's life after he was shot in the chest by Johnson.

usually occurred in similar situations. Whatever the source of Johnson's courage, he did not need to bolster it with war cries.

Inspector Eames changed his tactics. Except for a small stand of trees on one side the cabin was centered in a clearing across which any advance would have to be made. Here and there a tree provided barely adequate cover. As a posse member remarked later: "You never realize how skinny a tree is until you are trying to hide behind it."

The Inspector placed his men behind the river bank around three sides of the clearing. He himself went over the top, followed by Constables Millen and McDowell. From other points the three trappers — Ernest Sutherland, Carl Gardlund and Knut Lang — converged on the cabin. Hardly had they cleared the river bank when Johnson began to shoot rapidly from almost ground level. It appeared to McDowell that since his last trip, Johnson had poked loopholes through the frozen mud used to chink the log walls. From them he could cover every approach. Since the cabin itself was scarcely larger than a pool table, Johnson was able to move quickly from point to point and snap shots in the direction of threatened attack. As was later discovered he had sawn off the butt and barrel of his shotgun and .22 rifle, and was effectively using these short range weapons.

The posse's bullets seemed to have no effect on the log walls, and unless they could make an opening, Johnson appeared to have the advantage. With little cover, the six attackers began a series of darting raids on the cabin, trying to get close enough to batter down the door with rifle butts as they raced past the cabin. Finally, seizing a moment when Johnson was oc-

Trapper K.H. "Knut" Lang, one of the men who faced Johnson's bullets to lob dynamite at his cabin.

20

cupied on the other side of the cabin, Gardlund and Lang managed to jar the door loose. Through the opening Lang saw Johnson crouching in the hole he had dug. The trapper spun round and opened fire, shooting from both hands, as the men ducked for cover. Lang reported to Eames that Johnson had an automatic in each hand, but it is more likely that these were the sawed-off shotgun and .22 rifle.

Their first efforts repulsed, the police then brought up the dog teams and made camp below the river bank. They could hear Johnson moving about in his cabin, firmly closing the door.

With the early arrival of darkness, the posse lit flares and kept a constant vigil on the cabin. Johnson appeared to have an inexhaustible supply of ammunition, for he fired at the slightest movement above the river bank.

Inspector Eames realized from Lang's brief description of the cabin's interior that it would be difficult to dislodge Johnson by riddling the structure with bullets. He gave orders for the dynamite to be thawed — a tricky business even under ideal conditions. Eames then attempted to dislodge the logs by exploding charges against them in the manner of a grenade attack. Unfortunately, most of the charges failed to explode and those that did made no impression on the walls.

Towards midnight, Knut Lang volunteered to toss a large charge onto the roof, hoping to weaken the cabin. A larger bomb was prepared. While other members of the posse began a cross-fire on the cabin to drive Johnson from his loopholes, Lang ran over the frozen bank to the cabin and tossed the dynamite onto the roof. The explosion caused scarcely a moment's interruption in the trapper's return fire and Lang had to scramble fast for cover. Beyond creating a small hole in the roof and blowing off the tin smokestack, the dynamite proved ineffective.

By 3 a.m. Inspector Eames, conscious that his party was suffering from the intense cold and lack of sleep, and that supplies were running low for the dogs, decided to make one last attempt. The men had laid siege to the wilderness "fort" for nearly fifteen hours and its defender appeared as secure, determined and defiant as in the beginning.

Eames had the rest of the dynamite thawed. Poised on the edge of the river bank with trapper Gardlund behind him, Eames arched the bundle of explosives across the clearing. His throw was perfect. The charge exploded against the cabin with a brilliant flash and thunderous crack.

Certain that the blast must have stunned Johnson, if only momentarily, Eames and Gardlund charged. They had agreed that if the dynamite blasted down the door, Gardlund would try to blind Johnson with a spotlight, while Eames would disarm him before he could recover. Gardlund switched on the light, revealing a tangled mass of logs. But Johnson had been neither injured nor stunned by the dynamite blast — although the cabin had almost collapsed around him. He immediately opened fire. A well-aimed shot smashed the light from Gardlund's hand and sent Eames and the trapper back to the river bank.

It was obvious to the Inspector that the siege could not continue under the circumstances. After a short rest — the first his men had taken in eighteen hours — he led them from the scene. Two days later, the posse reached Aklavik and relief from the punishing cold.

Death of A Constable

The first news of the drama in the Northwest Territories reached the public on January 6, 1932, when Canadian Press news service carried a dispatch giving scanty details of the near fatal wounding of Constable King. Somewhere along the line, an enthusiastic reporter or editor decided that the episode smacked of "cabin-fever" and wrote of Johnson as a "crazed" and "demented man."

When a week later word reached the outside world via radio that Johnson had withstood the siege of the posse under Inspector Eames, the public's interest was immediately rivetted on the north. As often happens when authority is pitted against an individual, however, the public had a great deal of sympathy for Johnson and secretly admired his stand against the police. Many doubted that he was crazed or demented.

Sensing the story of the decade, newspaper reporters began to search.

Although Johnson's cabin was virtually demolished by the dynamite blast, he was uninjured.

Who was Albert Johnson? Where did he come from? What took him north and what brought on the duel with the police? Despite later evidence to the contrary, popular writers would christen Johnson, "The Mad Trapper of Rat River."

But while newsmen were trying to learn Johnson's identity, at Aklavik priority preparations were underway for a second, larger posse. After only two days of rest, Constable Millen left Aklavik and followed the now familiar trail to Rat River. With him went Carl Gardlund. His orders were to camp some distance from the cabin and determine if Johnson was still there.

Their second day out of Aklavik, Millen and Gardlund ran into an Arctic blizzard that lasted three days. Under its cover they approached close to the cabin and in daylight were able to assess the damage.

The front wall had been blown in and the roof with its heavy overlay of sod had almost collapsed. They found it difficult to believe that Johnson had survived. Nevertheless, Johnson had not only survived, he had left — probably under cover of the blizzard.

Close examination of the cabin revealed nothing. There were no letters, papers or documents that gave any indication of Johnson's past, or his plans. Further searching revealed his canoe and cache of supplies. Again, there was nothing in the cache to give them a clue to his identity and the blizzard had obliterated all signs of any trail Johnson left in his flight.

After finding the shack of a Loucheux Indian family in the vicinity, Constable Millen despatched the man with a note to Inspector Eames informing him of Johnson's departure. Then, with the experienced Carl Gardlund he began a series of forays during calm spells in the fitful blizzard to try to determine which direction the fugitive had taken.

While Millen and Gardlund scoured the inhospitable region, Aklavik was a bustle of activity. Alerted by radio, most of the men and women of the district fled their isolated cabins to seek the safety of police headquarters. Many trappers volunteered their services in tracking down the outlaw of Rat River. From them Inspector Eames chose John Parsons, an ex-member of the force, Frank Carmichael, and Noel Verville, a rough, tough trapper whose love of bar-room brawls was a community by-word. Others in the party included Ernest Sutherland and the always-smiling Special Constable Sittichiulis — already veterans of the Rat River battle — and two members of the Royal Canadian Signals stationed at Aklavik. They were Quartermaster Sergeant R.F. Riddell and Staff Sergeant Earl Hersey, who brought with them a two-way radio to improve communications between the posse and headquarters. It was the first time a radio had been used for police communications, although for Hersey the historic event would have nearly tragic consequences when he was felled by Johnson's deadly shooting.

The group left Aklavik on January 16 but soon encountered the blizzard that was hampering Millen and Gardlund. Despite the storm they fought their way through the wind-whipped snow to the mouth of the Rat River in two days. There they were met by Millen's messenger and learned for the first time that Johnson had left his cabin and was somewhere in the swirling whiteness.

A base camp was established 15 km (9 miles) east of Johnson's cabin and for the next four days the party scoured the defiles of Rat River Canyon hoping to pick up some trace of the fugitive's trail. Deserted cabins and clumps of trees had to be approached with extreme caution, slowing the search.

Constable Millen and Gardlund joined the party the next day, reporting that they had found no sign of Johnson's trail. Millen had located Johnson's trap lines, but evidently the trapper had not visited them for some time. A small band of Loucheux Indians was recruited to speed up the search but even the addition of eleven of their number failed to turn up any definite clue to the fugitive's passage. The blizzard, while a hardship to the outlaw, was also an advantage since it obliterated all tracks.

By January 21, with supplies for men and dogs again running low,

Eames dismissed the Indians and reconsidered his position. There were supplies for about four more days of search with the large party. But by withdrawing most of the men and allocating greater supplies to an advance party, the search could continue for another ten days.

Eames decided upon the latter course and detailed the experienced Constable Millen to continue the search. His choice was probably influenced by the fact that the young constable was the only one who could accurately identify Johnson if he were encountered. Millen was joined by Gardlund, trapper Noel Verville and Staff Sergeant Riddell in charge of the radio.

Plagued by the problem of logistics, Inspector Eames decided to establish a base camp on the Rat River and left Hersey there while he returned to Aklavik to regroup and freight in supplies for a prolonged search.

Constable Millen and his men made their way to Johnson's shattered cabin and finally found faint traces of a trail at a portage near where the Bear River joins the Rat. Like most men in the north, Johnson had fashioned his own snowshoes which left tracks as individual and distinctive as fingerprints. With extreme difficulty because of the rugged terrain and numbing sub-zero temperatures, the four men managed to follow the trail westward into the foothills of the Richardson Mountains that separated the Northwest Territories from the Yukon. Their radio equipment proved useless because the intense cold froze the batteries and they were seldom in camp long enough to thaw them out.

Then in the higher country towards which Johnson appeared to be

Staff Sergeant H.F. "Earl" Hersey. He was fortunate to live after being wounded by Johnson during the confrontation on the Eagle River.

heading they lost the trail completely. They were still searching for it when an Indian runner arrived with the message that two shots had been heard the day before in the vicinity of Bear River. Suspecting that it might have been Johnson replenishing his food supply, the four-man posse retraced its steps to the river country. There a fresh fall of snow enabled them to pick up the trail made by Johnson's distinctive snowshoes. Obviously the fugitive had doubled back from the open, rocky terrain of the foothills and regained the trees fringing the river banks.

Shortly after daybreak on January 30, the four men followed the tracks up a small creek (now called Millen Creek) which empties into the Rat River about one mile north of the confluence of the Rat and Barrier Rivers. They followed the trail up the creek for 8 km (5 miles) to where it led into a triangular clump of trees. Closer examination revealed that there were no tracks leading out of the tangle of trees and large boulders.

The posse split up. Riddell and Gardlund crossed the creek bed below Johnson's hiding spot and circled to a point on the river bank above the cluster of trees. From this vantage they could look down into a ravine. Though they could not see Johnson, they could hear someone coughing occasionally. If it were the fugitive, he had chosen his camp well for the fallen tree trunks and large smooth boulders provided a natural fortification.

Once Gardlund and Riddell were in position, Constable Millen and Verville descended the slope and cautiously approached the camp.

Without warning, Johnson reacted to their stealthy approach. As Millen passed an opening in the trees, Johnson fired at him with his .30-30

Quarter Master Sergeant R.F. Riddell of the Royal Canadian Corps of Signals.

rifle. In that fleeting instance, Carl Gardlund caught a glimpse of Johnson and snapped a shot at him. When Johnson dropped out of sight, Gardlund thought that he might have been hit.

Uninjured, Constable Millen joined his companions in pouring a rapid, if blind, fire into the concealed position. When there was no reply from Johnson, the conviction grew that Gardlund's first shot had found its mark, but still they made no move against the shelter. Verville and Riddell were new to this deadly game, but Millen and Gardlund were veterans of the cabin siege and knew first-hand the cunning tactics of their man. Despite the fact that outside news reports were referring to Johnson as a demented man, they knew that he was desperate, dangerous and in full possession of his mental faculties.

As a precaution the men waited for over two hours, during which time there was no sign of movement from Johnson's improvised shelter. Believing Johnson to be dead or too seriously injured to resist, Constable Millen led his men closer.

"When we were within about 25 yards," Sergeant Riddell recalled, "Johnson suddenly sprang up and fired on us."

While his companions scrambled for cover, Edgar Millen stood his ground. It seemed inevitable that Millen and Johnson should meet face to face again. One a desperate man who appeared to cherish an ancient grudge against the police, the other a dedicated man of the north, a law officer doing his duty to protect the public.

For a moment they faced each other. Millen coolly and deliberately fired two shots. Johnson replied with three from his rifle. Constable Millen fell.

When Sergeant Riddell regained the lip of the ravine a short distance away, he saw Millen lying inert in the snow. There was no sign of the trapper.

Riddell and Verville, protecting themselves against further outburst from Johnson's deadly rifle which had again fallen silent, kept up a steady sniper fire on the thicket. Gardlund, bravely slithering forward on his stomach, managed to reach the fallen Millen. He tied the Constable's boot laces together and used them as a handle to pull the Mountie back over the bank. A quick examination showed that Constable Millen was dead.

With daylight already fading, the three remaining members of the party took turns firing into the thicket, hoping to get Johnson to show himself again, or to disable him with a ricochet. Again, however, the wily fugitive resorted to his stratagem of silence.

As Riddell had the fastest dog team, they decided he should return to Aklavik with news of Millen's death. He set off into the gathering Arctic darkness, while Gardlund and Verville started work on a pole platform to protect Millen's body from prowling animals. That completed, they settled down to keep watch on Johnson's silent camp.

A short distance from Johnson's cabin, Riddell met Staff Sergeant Hersey and Special Constable Sittichiulis who were on their way to relieve the Millen party. On hearing of Millen's death, Hersey decided to continue on to join Verville and Gardlund, while Sittichiulis accompanied Riddell to Aklavik.

Pursuit in the Frozen Wilderness

When Inspector Eames learned of Millen's tragic death he immediately sent Ernest Sutherland, Special Constable Hatting and Reverend Thomas Murry to reinforce the party keeping vigil over Johnson's hiding place.

Although Eames was still not completely satisfied with his efforts to build up a supply base on the Rat River, he felt impelled by the growing seriousness of the situation to move there on February 2 with a third large posse. Thus far Johnson had only fought when attacked or cornered, but there was no assurance he might not attack a small party of police if he

found an advantage. His coolness under fire and careful use of ammunition suggested possible military or police background. Eames entirely discounted the press theory that Johnson was mad. "I note in press reports that Johnson is referred to as 'the demented trapper'," he later wrote in his official report. "On the contrary, he showed himself to be an extremely shrewd and resolute man, capable of quick thought and action. A tough and desperate character."

To complicate the Inspector's job, atmospheric conditions caused a

The Ballanca and her crew wait out a snow storm during the search for Johnson. At times wind swirled snow 300 m (1,000 ft.) into the air.

deterioration in radio communications. Nevertheless, an alert was broadcast repeatedly for volunteers to assemble at Fort McPherson or Blake's post on the Husky River.

On February 2, 1932, Eames left Aklavik with Riddell, Sittichiulis and three trappers — ex-constable Constant Ethier, Peter Strandberg and Ernest Maring. Detouring by way of Fort McPherson, he added Knut Lang and Frank Carmichael, and at Blake's post, collected August Tardiff and John Greenland. Although he was already beginning to suffer from the illness that would kill him three years later, Arthur Blake insisted on accompanying them.

Owing to heavy winds and frequent blizzards travel was so difficult that the posse had to break trail for the dogs between Blake's post as far up the Rat River as its confluence with the Barrier. At that camp, Eames learned by wireless that an airplane he requested to assist in the manhunt had left Edmonton February 3. But he realized that with 2,900 km (1,800 miles) to cover, short flying hours and constant storms, it would be some time before its help could be counted on.

Two days later the main posse linked up with the advance party at the creek where Constable Edgar Millen had been slain. At that point there were at least seventeen men actively engaged in tracking Johnson and of them, only one was a regular policeman.

For the first time since Millen's death an advance was made on Johnson's camp. No one was surprised to find, however, that he had escaped

Ex-RCMP officer C. Jack Ethier during the manhunt.

again, either under cover of darkness or during one of the frequent storms that covered the area during the past week. The absence of blood in the camp indicated that he was not wounded, despite the furious fusillade the Millen party had poured into his hideout. Again, there was nothing to indicate Johnson's background.

The posse spent that day searching the ravine but drifting snow wiped out all trace of the elusive trapper. From the ravine the search extended westward towards the foothills of the Richardson Mountains which were serated with numerous creeks, each bordered with ribbons of stunted trees. The country was bleak frozen tundra, the snow packed and hardened by the ceaseless winds which quickly obliterated any tracks.

While the main search focussed along the Barrier River, small parties spread out in all directions. On February 6 one of these parties found Johnson's tracks along the bed of a small creek. With growing optimism they followed the tracks but their enthusiasm waned when the tracks ascended the bank of the creek and disappeared in the frozen tundra.

A day later, another trail was located in a creek bed some 6 km (4 miles) away, paralleling the first and travelling in the same direction. Far from fleeing the area, Johnson seemed to be playing hide and seek with his pursuers. On another occasion, two parties of trackers, following two individual sets of prints, suddenly found themselves face to face. They then realized that Johnson was wearing his snowshoes backwards in a further effort to deceive them.

With two or three days head start, Johnson had ample opportunity, especially with his skill at concealing his trail, to vanish completely from the district. But for some unknown reason he lingered in the area, circling back frequently on his trail and at times obviously watching the pursuit. Was he waiting for an opportunity to ambush an unwary party, or simply demonstrating his superiority?

Meanwhile, in response to Inspector Eames' request for aerial assistance an aeroplane had left Edmonton. Aboard were pilot Captain W.R. "Wop" May, his mechanic, Jack Bowen, and Constable William S. Carter who knew the Rat River district intimately.

Wop May, one of the original bush pilots who opened the northland, was already a northern legend. (See page 82.) Born in Carberry, Manitoba, in 1896, May enlisted in the Royal Flying Corps during World War One and on his first mission over enemy lines in 1918 decoyed Germany's ace, Baron von Richthofen, into the guns of a fellow pilot, Roy Brown. May himself went on to shoot down thirteen enemy planes and establish himself as a Canadian ace. He came out of the war with the Distinguished Flying Cross, a captain's rank, and a life-long love of flying.

Captain May flew north in a Canadian Airways black and orange Bellanca monoplane by way of Fort Smith and Arctic Red River. After several futile attempts to locate Inspector Eames' camp, the trio continued to Aklavik. The next day May found the Eames posse on the Barrier River. After delivering Constable Carter, he took off with Staff Sergeant Riddell to try to locate Johnson's trail from the air.

The plane covered in minutes an area that took the posse a day or more of difficult land travel. Riddell was able to spot and eliminate leads and

W.R. Wop May whose flying skill saved Hersey's life. Of the Johnson episode, May recalled: "My job was to fly over his tracks and find his tent and then fly back and direct the police and the dog teams the quickest way to get him . . . ."

false leads. As a pattern developed, it appeared that Johnson had never been far from his pursuers.

"At one place a trail led off, heading directly for the divide (between the Yukon and the Territories), and also another trail, just as fresh looking, continued on up the Barrier River. It ended abruptly." Riddell recalled. "Later on we discovered another faint trail leading from this and ending in a circle. Evidently Johnson had circled back on his own tracks and camped for the night just off his main trail so that he could watch it . . . . "

Camp was moved up to the junction of these two trails and the foot search intensified. The airplane shortened travel time to Aklavik to under an hour instead of over two days, and Inspector Eames used May's machine to freight in a steady stream of supplies. On Monday, February 8, May flew in 700 pounds of food and took out Constable Millen's body.

That same day searchers found a third set of tracks on another creek paralleling the other two main trails. This discovery gave them added proof of Johnson's amazing stamina. But despite all the tracks, the plane and some twenty experienced men scouring the countryside, the posse appeared no closer to cornering their dangerous adversary. Johnson was out-thinking, out-running and out-enduring his enemies.

That afternoon surprise reinforcements arrived at the Eames camp. As a result of orders from Ottawa headquarters, the officer commanding the RCMP in the Yukon had broadcast a message alerting all patrols in the district of the situation that existed in the Northwest Territories. As a result Constable Sidney W. May (no relation to Wop May) led a party of five volunteers from the police outpost of Old Crow on the Bell River over 200 km (120 miles) west of the search area. In his party were trappers Frank Jackson and Frank Hogg, and two Indian volunteers.

Another howling blizzard swept the area, not only grounding the plane at Aklavik but almost burying it beneath drifting snow. By next day, however, May was again air borne. In the meantime, a small patrol led by newcomer Constable May went as far as timberline on the Barrier River and discovered tracks made by Johnson. They were clearly leading into the Richardson Mountains and towards the Yukon divide.

Outwardly it appeared that the outlaw had either tired of teasing his pursuers or, unable to cope with the menace posed by the airplane, was fleeing westwards towards Alaska. But there was still the possibility that these tracks were another diversion and that Johnson was still in the area.

The Indians in the posse were particularly certain that Johnson was still on the east side of the divide. They assured Inspector Eames that no one could cross the 1,500 m (5,000 ft.) range of mountains alone in winter. Well aware of Johnson's incredible endurance and strength, Eames was just as certain that while the fugitive might not be able to cross the snow-clogged mountain pass at the head of the Barrier River, he certainly had the courage to make an attempt.

Once again, however, the Inspector's need for supplies gave Johnson a respite. Eames was forced to withdraw his huge posse from the Barrier River and return to base camp on the Rat — leaving only a small party under Constable May to watch for Johnson. For three days Eames impatiently waited while Wop May and Bowen flew in load after load of supplies.

Shoot-out
on the Eagle River

As the supply build-up continued on the fringe of the Arctic, public interest from Victoria on the Pacific Coast to St. John's on the Atlantic became more intense. Fed on a daily diet of Depression news, and frightened by the prospect of unemployment, people welcomed the diversion of a dramatic manhunt in the north. Information by radio and newspaper was eagerly awaited.

The Eagle River with Johnson lying on the ice in the center of the channel and firing on the posse. The ox-bow course of the river is shown in the photo taken by pilot Wop May.

The chief factor which helped create and sustain the public's interest was the lack of concrete information. The news that filtered from Aklavik, though hampered by poor radio communications, was remarkably accurate, but there was little of it. Days passed without new information.

Then on February 11, 1932, a photograph of Albert Johnson appeared on the front page of newspapers across the country. The photo was that of a trapper complete with fur hat. While it took little imagination to picture him snowshoeing across the tundra with a rifle slung across his back, there was little biographical material with the photo. It was identified simply as Albert Johnson, the trapper who had killed Constable Millen. Readers surmised that complete details would be given in later editions.

The additional information never did appear. Although the man in the fur cap was Albert Johnson, and he had been a trapper in the Northwest Territories, he was neither "demented" nor had he killed anybody. Albert Johnson of Princeton, B.C., marched angrily into the offices of a large Vancouver newspaper and demanded retraction of both photo and story. The offending photograph quickly disappeared from the newspapers from Victoria to Montreal.

In the Arctic, meanwhile, the "other Albert Johnson" had disappeared completely. The advance party under Constable Sidney May had not located any further trace of the fugitive after the initial discovery of his tracks leading to the Barrier River pass. The lack of firewood, scarcity of game and absence of a clearly marked trail through the pass convinced most that Johnson would not try it. All of them underestimated the remarkable stamina of the trapper. On February 12 Peter Alexei, an Indian from La Pierre House on the west flank of the Richardson Mountains, mushed into the police camp to inform Inspector Eames that there were strange snowshoe tracks only a short distance from La Pierre House. Furthermore, they fitted the radio description of Johnson's tracks.

Inspector Eames was amazed. If this report were true, it meant that Johnson had travelled 145 km (90 miles) in the heart of a blizzard in less than three days. In addition, he had crossed a mountain pass said to be impenetrable in winter.

In view of this report, the Inspector decided upon a two-fold approach. In the event that Johnson might try to slip back over the pass, Eames had Wop May freight in eight pairs of snowshoes suitable for soft snow. With them he out-fitted a party under Constable May to follow Johnson's route through the pass itself. Then with Sergeant Riddell and Carl Gardlund, Eames flew to La Pierre House to establish new search headquarters.

The three found entirely different climatic conditions on the western side of the Divide. Where the frozen tundra on the Rat River had provided ample snow-free terrain over which Johnson could travel without leaving prints, the western slopes and foothills were heavy with snow that retained tracks even under blowing conditions. The weather was warmer but dense fogs presented much the same visibility problem as had the blizzards along the Barrier River. The problems caused by the blizzard conditions were later described by Quartermaster Sergeant Riddell who flew with May to assist in finding the trail: ". . . the heavy winds which at times blew drifting snow as high as a thousand feet, prevented the plane from making observations and also being able to land and connect with the ground party . . . ."

Despite these inclement conditions, May successfully moved his makeshift flying field base from Aklavik to La Pierre House. On February 14 he took off at 3.05 p.m. in the already waning daylight and almost immediately located a snowshoe trail left by Johnson just south of the trading post. He followed it down the Bell River, noting that Johnson seemed to have made no effort to deviate from a straight line. He appeared to be heading due west. Suddenly, the trail was obliterated by thousands of caribou hoof prints. Johnson had overtaken a herd of caribou and travelled with the animals, effectively concealing his route.

May followed the caribou tracks to the mouth of the Eagle River, then turned back, realizing that Johnson could not be far away. As May later recalled: "We tried to get him to shoot at us, so as to find his position, but he wouldn't."

Only fifteen minutes after take-off, May was back at La Pierre House, detailing his discovery to Inspector Eames. In that quarter-hour he had accomplished what might have taken the foot posse days to achieve. Johnson's four-day advantage gained by crossing the formidable Barrier River Pass had been slashed to only one.

Dense fog shrouded the area the following day, grounding the plane. Towards late afternoon, however, the search party under Constable Sidney May arrived. The Constable reported that they had located several of Johnson's camps in the pass, but again careful search had failed to uncover any clues to his identity or eventual destination. Even with eight men in the party, they had found the traverse "one hell of a trip," and paid grudging respect to the man who had done it alone.

Although the region was still covered with fog the next day, Inspector Eames nevertheless headed his searchers to the junction of the Bell and Eagle Rivers. Here they found traces of a trail heading southwest on the Eagle River, a wide, serpentine stream that at places doubled back on itself

The Bellanca with Wop May, left, and mechanic Jack Bowen.

37

so that the posse were heading south one hour, north the next.

Adding urgency to the search was the fact that Johnson's present direction would take him near the isolated cabin of a trader named Barnstrum, although no one knew its exact location. Eames had planned to have Captain May cruise the area that day to locate the cabin from the air and alert its occupant, but the plane was still grounded by fog.

The possibility that Johnson might find the cabin and make another desperate stand like his siege on the Rat River was not a prospect Inspector Eames relished. With this thought foremost, the men kept searching, eliminating every false trail. Gardlund and Riddell were detailed to carefully mark the true trail for Wop May to follow when the fog lifted. Ahead, somewhere, Albert Johnson pressed on, laying out trail and counter trail. Unable to light a fire lest it led the posse to him, unable to kill for food lest the sound of his rifle revealed his presence, he survived by snaring squirrels and brewing tea over miniature fires concealed in tiny caves in the snow-crusted river banks. From time to time he climbed trees to survey his back trail or lay out a course ahead.

By Tuesday evening Johnson's tracks appeared to be less than twenty-four hours old. Inspector Eames was confident that if Johnson followed his usual pattern of travelling two false miles for every true mile, they would come upon him the next day.

The searchers broke camp before dawn next morning, February 17, easily following the tracks despite the darkness. When dawn came, clear and fogless, the freshness of the tracks indicated that they were rapidly

Sergeant C. Neary.

38

gaining on Johnson. Inspector Eames did not then realize how close was a sudden, dramatic confrontation between hunted and the hunters.

Shortly before noon, Johnson left the frozen Eagle River and climbed a tree on the bank. From this vantage point he spotted the dark blotches of the oxbow course of the river. Johnson believed that the posse was ahead of him and moving away to the south. It was actually heading towards another bend which made the river again head north.

Johnson returned to the river ice and began to backtrack southward, away, he mistakenly thought, from the police party. He covered about half a mile, turned a bend then stopped abruptly. Some 300 yards away, heading straight for him, were two dog teams. Driving the lead toboggan was Staff Sergeant Earl Hersey. He, too, was startled as he rounded the same bend to discover the elusive trapper coming towards him.

Johnson was the first to react. Quickly he laced on his snowshoes. By the time Hersey had stopped the dogs and snatched a rifle, Johnson had reached the comparative shelter of the bank. Hersey and Verville, driver of the second toboggan, opened fire at long range. Johnson returned the fire, his main target Hersey who was kneeling in the open. One bullet caught the sergeant. As he fell, Johnson swung his deadly rifle at Verville. By now, however, the rest of the twelve-man posse had arrived with Carl Gardlund and Frank Johnson reaching the bank and moving upward on both sides of the stream.

Albert Johnson left the shelter of the bank which was too steep to climb and began running back along the river. Despite his emaciated condition, the weight of his pack and his ungainly snowshoes, he pulled away from the posse. His objective was the opposite bank where the incline was less steep and underbrush offered him protection. But a burst of rifle fire rippled the snow around him. In mid-river he suddenly dropped.

Burrowing into a snow drift, he dragged his pack in front of him and methodically began to return the fire. There was no panic, no shout of defiance, no acceptance of the inevitable. Just Johnson with his supreme self-confidence determined to emerge the victor.

The posse moved towards him along the tree-studded banks. They called repeatedly for his surrender but also maintained a steady sniper fire. Then some of the group gained positions on the banks overlooking Johnson's snow trench. From then Johnson's end was assured.

Though hit repeatedly, Johnson fought on. He was lying on his side reloading his rifle when a bullet struck him in the spine. His desperate resistance ended.

May, swooping overhead, saw Johnson's sprawled figure, his arm outslung, rifle unattended. The pilot dipped his wings to signal the end and circled to land on the frozen river. At 12.10 p.m. on February 17, 1932, Inspector Eames' posse moved in to surround Johnson's body. Among wounds was a hole blown in his hip when one of the rifle bullets exploded ammunition in his pocket. His frozen, emaciated face was twisted into a horrible grimace, teeth looking like fangs through his beard. Members of the posse never forgot the face with its half-open eyes which stared at them in hate and lips curled back in the most terrible sneer that any of them had ever seen.

Closing the Case

Inspector Eames' duties were not over with the death of Albert Johnson. His first job was to get the wounded Hersey to Aklavik. Sergeant Riddell later told a special correspondent for the *Edmonton Journal:* ". . . as soon as the firing ceased, I dashed over to Hersey, followed by the rest of the party, and to my joy found he was still alive. It at first appeared that he had been hit three times as he was bleeding from the knee, the arm, and the chest. However, it was later found that one bullet had caused all three wounds. As Hersey was kneeling on his right knee with his left elbow resting on his left knee, the bullet had grazed the knee cap, entered the elbow, came out the upper arm, and into his chest."

First aid was rendered. Then Wop May and Riddell carried Hersey aboard the plane. It was probably one of May's most nerve-wracking

flights. Aware that Hersey was not dressed to survive the bitterly cold flight over the Richardson Mountains, he had to fly his plane close to the ground, expertly twisting and swerving through the narrow defiles of McDouglas Pass. Riddell sat on the floor with Hersey's head in his lap, trying to ignore the craggy rock bluffs skimming past the wing tips.

Of the flight, May was to recall: "We covered the 130 miles in an hour and forty minutes from the time he was hit. We nearly went through the mountains on that trip. There was fog and snow and I don't know how we got through. If we had been a quarter of an hour later the man would have bled to death."

With Hersey on his way to the expert care of Dr. Urquhart, Eames dispatched a party up river to Barnstrum's cabin to ensure that he had not

Rugged peaks to 2,450 m (8,000 ft.) confronted Wop May when he flew the gravely wounded Hersey to the doctor at Aklavik, forcing him to weave through the mountains rather than flying over them.

already fallen to Johnson's guns. It was this party that found the tree Johnson had climbed only minutes before and from which he had made his only — and final — miscalculation.

Then Eames with the remainder of the posse and Johnson's emaciated, bullet-ridden body on Verville's toboggan, returned to La Pierre House. The following day Wop May flew the dead man's remains and his few possesions to Aklavik.

News of the search's outcome soon reached the rest of the country. On February 20 the following account appeared in the *Edmonton Journal:* "AKLAVIK, N.W.T., Feb. 19. — All is quiet on the northern front as Albert Johnson's bullet-riddled, half-starved body lies in police barracks here. Meantime Staff Sergeant E.F. Hersey, of the Royal Canadian Signals Corps who was wounded by Johnson in his last fight, is reported improving.

"In the same aeroplane which materially aided in bringing him to his death Johnson's body was flown here yesterday. Pilot W.R. 'Wop' May left the Eagle river battle ground right after Johnson was shot down Wednesday and brought Hersey to hospital here. He covered the 125 miles in 45 minutes.

"Yesterday May returned to the scene and brought in Johnson's body. The round trip took four hours. Inspector E.A. Eames of the Royal Canadian Mounted Police who directed the chase of the supposedly mad trapper returned in the aeroplane and the rest of the pursuit party is coming back by dog team.

Post Rejoices

"This tiny Arctic trading post rejoiced today, glad its terrorist bad man, Albert Johnson, is dead and glad young Hersey, hero of the mad trapper's last-stand-battle on the snowy tundras of the Yukon, is going to recover from bullet wounds.

"Wounded in the final gun-fight between the desperate, sharp-shooting Rat River hermit and the police-trapper posse which finally caught up with him after a three weeks' chase, Hersey was virtually out of danger. He was rushed here immediately by aeroplane after Johnson shot him down and then himself fell dead before a withering return fire.

"A bullet which entered his chest on the left side was discovered yesterday to be located in the right side of his back, about two and a half inches from the spine. Dr. J.A. Urquhart, attending physician, said it can be easily removed. Hersey suffered from shock at first but is now resting easily and only danger of pneumonia or infection remains.

Trappers' Wives To Return

"Tension that had hung over the far north lifted with word Johnson had been killed by the posse seeking him for the murder of a Royal Canadian Mounted Police constable and wounding of another. Trappers' wives who came here many miles from their lonely cabins in scattered sections of the Arctic circle country, prepared to return.

"The women swarmed into Aklavik when they learned more than a month ago that the hermit trapper had broken loose from his strange shack in the Rat River area after wounding Constable A.W. King and withstanding a 15-hour shell and dynamite assault by police. Fearful Johnson might come upon their cabins while their husbands were out on the trap lines, the womenfolk remained here for the duration of the search."

The inquest at Aklavik into Johnson's death resulted in the following verdict: "We, the jury, find that the man known as Albert Johnson came to his death from concentrated rifle fire from a party composed of members of the Royal Canadian Mounted Police and others, Johnson having been called upon to surrender by several members of the party and still deliberately resisted arrest, we are satisfied that no responsibility rests with any member of the party, or the party as a whole. We are further satisfied from the evidence that the party had no other means of effecting Johnson's capture except by the method employed."

Johnson was buried in the Aklavik cemetery. In a land where trees are scarce, someone in later years dragged a large, forked tree trunk to the site and on one limb painted the initial "A"; on the other, "J."

Another interment took place on February 29, 1932. Constable Edgar Millen was buried with full military honors in an impressive ceremony at Edmonton's Beechmont Cemetery. Twenty-nine years later a wooden cairn was erected on the site where Constable Millen was gunned down. In 1968 Edmonton belatedly dedicated a small park to him.

Of others involved in the chase, Inspector Eames left the north in 1933 and in the following years served in many parts of Canada. He retired in 1946 as Assistant Commissioner after thirty-three years with the Force. He died in Vancouver in 1965 just after his 81st birthday.

Noel Verville, one of the dog team drivers in the final chase, left the

Albert Johnson's grave at Aklavik. The sign is inscribed: "Albert Johnson arrived in Ross River Aug. 21, 1927. Complaints of local trappers brought the RCMP on him. He shot two officers and became a fugitive of the law with howling huskies, dangerous trails, frozen nights. The posse finally caught up with him. He was killed up the Eagle River, Feb. 17, 1932."

Constable Edgar Millen (inset) was killed by Albert Johnson on the Rat River. Millen was buried with full military honours in Edmonton's Beechmont Cemetery on February 29, 1932. Below, the marker on the creek where Constable Millen was killed.

ON THIS SITE
CST. E. MILLEN.
R.C.M.P. WAS
FATALLY SHOT
BY
ALBERT JOHNSON
"MAD TRAPPER"
JANUARY 30, 1932

Arctic in 1936 and for many years operated a hotel at Hudson Hope in B.C.'s Peace River country. He and his wife later settled in Victoria where he died in 1975 at 79.

Constable S.W. May, who led the party of five volunteers from the outpost at Old Crow and then followed Johnson's tracks through the Richardson Mountains, was discharged in 1935 — he broke the rules by getting married without consent. He worked for many years in the Yukon, then settled at Kamloops, B.C., where he died in 1973 at 68.

Constable Alfred King who came so close to death by Johnson's cowardly bullet remained with the force until 1953. Of the encounter he later recalled: "All I wanted to tell him was to leave the Indians' traps alone. Then all he had to do was get a trapper's license and he was all set."

King retired a corporal after twenty-seven years' service. Although he was never shot at again during his years in the Force, he was injured while serving with the Canadian Army in Italy during World War Two. After leaving the RCMP he worked as a security guard in Sarnia, Ontario, until his retirement.

The other participant in the northern saga who nearly died from a Johnson bullet was Staff Sergeant Earl Hersey. Like most of those involved in the search for Johnson, he grew weary of being interviewed and reading erroneous accounts of the shoot-out. One account, for instance, had Hersey dropping "face forward in the snow, mortally wounded."

In 1982 — fifty years after he fell "mortally wounded" — Hersey was interviewed by Canadian Press at his home in Barrie, Ontario. He recalled the sequence of events when he rounded a bend in the Eagle River with his team of seven huskies and saw Johnson coming towards him:

" 'As I approached, the Mad Trapper pulled his snowshoes from behind his back and I knew then who it was . . . . He put the snowshoes on and ran across the soft snow for the river bank. When he was halfway up, I got down on one knee and fired.

" 'I'm not the killer type — I aimed for his back. He carried a pack on his back with all his cooking utensils and blankets and gear. The shot knocked him off balance and down he came.'

"The Mad Trapper twice more tried to scramble up the steep bank and twice more fell, knocked off balance each time by Hersey's shots.

" 'I guess he got fed up. He reached for his gun and I thought, good, when he turns around I'll hit him in the shoulder. He had a .30-30, which is accurate to 100 yards, and I had a .303, which is accurate as all get out. I wasn't worried about him hitting me.

" 'I was down on one knee and being very, very careful of my aim. He pointed his gun straight at me and fired.'

"The bullet went through Hersey's knee, elbow and lungs," noted Canadian Press. "The posse raced to catch up. RCMP Insp. Alexander Eames called three times for the Mad Trapper to give up, but he kept firing from a trench in the snowbank, behind his backpack.

"The posse of Mounties, soldiers and Indians surrounded him. Eames gave the signal.

" 'He had 17 bullets in him,' Hersey says.

"But who was this mad trapper?"

(Staff Sergeant T. E. G. Shaw, retired editor of the RCMP's official magazine, RCMP Quarterly, *and an authority on the Johnson affair, feels that Albert Johnson and Arthur Nelson could well have been the same man. Among interesting information uncovered by Staff Sergeant Shaw was that the man known as Arthur Nelson had purchased six boxes of kidney pills at Mayo in the spring of 1931. Similar pills were found in Johnson's possession after his death.*

The amount of evidence amassed seems to point clearly to a relationship between Nelson and Johnson, but whether they were the same man is inconclusive, as indicated in the following article by Mr. Shaw.)

Who was Albert Johnson?

A stranger arrived at Ross River Post, Yukon Territory, August 21, 1927, and after a cursory look around, made his way to Taylor and Drury's Trading Store. Although not too much information was volunteered, trader Roy Buttle learned that the newcomer's name was Arthur Nelson, that he was a trapper, and that he intended to stay just long enough to build a boat.

The store-keeper said he would lend a hand and Nelson, although not too enthusiastic at first, finally accepted the offer. Roy Buttle sized the newcomer up fairly well, and in view of the fact he did not outwardly show too much curiosity or ask too many questions, the reticent Nelson did confide a few things to Buttle over the nine days it took them to put the boat together.

Roy Buttle found Nelson intelligent and highly rational in all conversations, but there was something in the man's make-up that made him seem odd. For one thing, Buttle was the only person around the Post the trapper would have anything to do with. He camped about half a mile from the settlement and openly showed that he welcomed no guests. Also, the Indians living around the Post were visibly afraid of the stranger and would have absolutely nothing to do with him.

This was not because Arthur Nelson was a towering giant of a man. Of average height, his well-proportioned frame packed about 170 pounds. His speech carried the trace of a Scandinavian accent and he seemed to walk

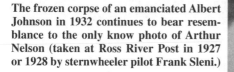

The frozen corpse of an emanciated Albert Johnson in 1932 continues to bear resemblance to the only know photo of Arthur Nelson (taken at Ross River Post in 1927 or 1928 by sternwheeler pilot Frank Sleni.)

with an habitual stoop as if he had been used to carrying an extremely heavy shoulder pack.

Nelson told Buttle he was an American and had been raised on a small farm in North Dakota. He appeared to be in his early 30s. He said he had reached Ross River via the headwaters of the Big and Little Salmon Rivers, having come from Teslin Lake. The previous winter he had been trapping in northern British Columbia in the area between Teslin and Dease Lakes. Buttle learned that Nelson had come to the Dease Lake area by way of the Stikine River and prior to that had worked at the mines at Anyox, B.C.

When the boat was finished, Nelson left the Post August 30, travelling up river. The Mounted Policeman at Ross River, Corporal Claude Tidd, himself a newcomer to the district the summer of 1927, was on patrol up the Pelly River at the time of Nelson's arrival. Although he returned a day or two before Nelson sailed up river, he did not meet the trapper, but did hear about him from Roy Buttle.

Arthur Nelson returned to Ross River Post June 16, 1928, and stayed around for a month until the trading store's annual supply boat arrived. He told Roy Buttle he had been trapping at Ross Lake during the winter. After the supplies came in, Nelson purchased a few provisions, a Savage .30–30 carbine and some .22 shells. He left suddenly in mid–July.

About a month later, three trappers — Oley Johnson, Norman Niddery and Oscar Erickson — were travelling up the south fork of the Stewart River. One morning as they were eating breakfast at Twin Falls, they noticed a stranger walking toward them. They invited him to join them but he refused, saying he had camped overnight upstream a piece and had already eaten. He told them his name was Arthur Nelson and asked the way to Keno in the Yukon.

Nelson said he had come from Ross River Post where he had built a boat and that he had hit the Stewart River above the Rogue River (a branch of the south fork of the Stewart). The three men did not see Nelson's boat as he was on foot when he approached their camp, and after learning the way to Keno, he hiked off in that direction.

Robert Levac who operated a trading store at Fraser Falls was the next man to come into contact with Nelson. The latter asked if he could stop over a day or two and Levac put him up in a spare cabin. Nelson wanted to get rid of some marten skins he had trapped, but Levac wouldn't buy them. He said he would bid on them, but suggested that Nelson take them to Mayo, in the Yukon, to sell.

Nelson kept pretty much to himself the two days he stayed at Fraser Falls, doing nothing but lie on his bunk. Occasionally he went into the store to buy something to eat, but he seemed moody and answered either a curt "yes" or "no" to any questions Levac asked. Before leaving, however, he did tell the trader that he had come from Ross River Post where he had built a boat the previous summer, but that it had been wrecked up the Ross River. When Nelson departed, he did so without saying a word to Levac.

A few days later, Arthur Nelson appeared in Mayo. One of the first things he did was to peddle his marten skins at the Taylor and Drury Store for $680. This transaction was completed between Nelson and Mr. W. H. Jeffrey of the firm on August 30, 1928. Nelson received this amount in cash through an arrangement between Taylor and Drury and the Bank of Montreal in Mayo, as the store did not have that much cash on hand.

Before the summer was out, Arthur Nelson joined trader James Mervyn who was ferrying his supplies up the Stewart River to his store at Lansing Creek. Mervyn put Nelson and his outfit off at the mouth of the south fork of the Stewart where the trapper spent the winter of 1928-29, and when Mervyn was returning to Mayo on his boat the following summer, he passed Nelson who was on a raft. The trader offered Nelson a ride, but the latter refused.

Prior to this (in March 1929) trapper Jack Alverson, who first met Nelson in Mayo in 1928, stayed one night at Nelson's cabin at the mouth of the south fork of the Stewart. Once again, however, Nelson was in one of his reticent moods and other than some talk about trapping, the only thing Alverson learned from Nelson was that he said he was Danish.

The next two winters, Arthur Nelson spent trapping in the Macmillan River district between Ross River Post and Mayo. On two occasions he visited the trading store at Russell Creek run by Mr. Zimmerlee. Although Zimmerlee did not see Nelson carrying firearms at any time, the trapper asked for some shot-gun shells on one occasion when he purchased supplies at the store.

In the spring of 1931, trapper P. Fredrickson of the Russell Post area sold a canoe to Arthur Nelson who paddled off up the Macmillan River. Later some Indians in the district found the canoe abandoned on the upper waters of that river. Nelson returned to Mayo shortly after leaving the Macmillan River area, stopping off long enough to pick up a few provisions, including an abundant quantity of kidney pills. Clerk Archie Currie of Binet's Store was rather startled when Nelson bought six boxes of pills, but Nelson was so uncommunicative that Currie thought twice about engaging the man in any conversation.

In May 1931, Arthur Nelson headed north to Keno. He stopped there briefly, making a small purchase in the store then managed by Joe Clifton and began walking north again. Frank Gillespie was having a cup of tea at the mouth of Crystal Creek one morning when Nelson happened upon his camp fire. Gillespie offered the traveller a cup, but Nelson refused, asking where the bridge on the McQuesten River was located as he said he was going to Haggart Creek. At the time, Nelson was laboring under the weight of a heavy shoulder pack.

"Snoose" Erickson and his partner, Sullivan, had a cabin on the McQuesten River. In May 1931 Nelson passed that way at noon one day carrying the heavy pack and a small rifle. Erickson asked the stranger to have lunch with them, but he curtly refused and kept walking in the direction of Eight-Mile Cabin near the head of the Beaver River in the Yukon.

From the head of the Beaver River, in May 1931 trapper Arthur Nelson seemingly vanished just as strangely as he had first suddenly appeared at Ross River Post nearly four years earlier.

*   *   *

On July 9, 1931, a stranger arrived at Fort McPherson, Northwest Territories, under rather unusual circumstances. This man drifted down the

Peel River from the direction of the Yukon on a raft consisting of three large logs to a spot about three miles above Fort McPherson. There he abandoned his crude craft and apparently with either little or no outfit, walked the remainder of the way into the Fort where he purchased supplies. He was said to be well stocked with cash.

This information was passed along to Inspector Alexander Neville Eames who commanded the Western Arctic Sub-District of the Royal Canadian Mounted Police (with headquarters at Aklavik, N.W.T.) by Bishop Geddes. Constable Edgar Millen, in charge of the Force's detachment at Arctic Red River, was sent instructions to interview the stranger.

(The events which unfurled after Constable Millen's meeting with the man who called himself Albert Johnson, the subsequent shooting of Constable King and murder of Constable Millen have already been related. At the end of the 48-day "Arctic Circle War" which resulted in the death of Johnson he was flown to Aklavik.)

All of Albert Johnson's effects were gathered up and checked. A total of $2,410 in cash was found on his corpse in denominations of $20, $50 and $100, as well as two United States $5 bills and one $10. There were also two small glass jars, one containing five pearls (later evaluated at $15) and five pieces of gold dental work worth $12.56.

Firearms found in his possession included a model 99 Savage .30-30 rifle, an Ivor Johnson sawed-off 16-gauge shot-gun and a .22 Winchester rifle, model 58 with cut-down stock. His supply of ammunition included thirty-nine .30-30 shells, eighty-four .22 shells and four 16-gauge shot-gun shells. There were other miscellaneous items, including packages containing a total of thirty-two pills.

Significantly enough, there was no trace of any written matter found either on Johnson's body, at his cabin or at any of the caches and camps he had made in the area of the Rat River. The two automatic pistols seen in Johnson's hand January 9 by Knut Lang were not located. An old canoe was at the cabin, and about 300 yards away a carefully concealed stage cache containing a quantity of provisions.

The task of identifying the man known as Albert Johnson was one that has never been successfully concluded. All the Force had to go on was that he had told Constable Millen in Fort McPherson that his name was Albert Johnson; the Indians complaining about trapline interference said they, too, believed this was his name.

Fingerprints taken from his corpse were sent to both Ottawa and Washington, D.C., but they were not linked to anyone with a criminal record in either country.

First reports of the other stranger in the lower Yukon who called himself Arthur Nelson came to the RCMP in August 1927. From the physical descriptions and "lone wolf" attitudes of the two men, it seemed likely that they were one and the same, but this has never been proved conclusively.

There are, however, some facts that make it seem likely Nelson and Johnson were identical. Sergeant James R. Purdie of the Dawson C.I.B. made inquiries at the banks to see if he could trace any of the currency found on Johnson's body. The Bank of Montreal traced two bills. One $50 bill was received at the bank as one of a shipment of 100 such bills on September 7, 1926, and the other — also a $50 bill — was one of 100 bills sent to the branch at Mayo on March 22, 1928.

There is no actual record of either Johnson or Nelson having been in Dawson although Corporal Arthur Thornthwaite of Old Crow Detachment in a report dated the same day Johnson was shot said that a local Indian gave a description of a man he worked with on the 12-Mile dredge out of Dawson in 1930. Except for this man having brown hair (Johnson's was light brown) they seemed identical. The Indian said the man called himself Al Johnson and left the district in the fall of 1930 after telling the Indian he was going to the Peel River district to trap alone.

It is reasonable to assume that Nelson received the second $50 bill from Mayo, as on August 30, 1928 — less than six months after the bill was sent to Mayo — Nelson received $680 in cash from the Bank of Montreal there from selling marten skins to the firm of Taylor and Drury.

The firearms found in Johnson's possession were not successfully traced due to company records having been destroyed. It is significant, however, that Arthur Nelson purchased a .30-30 Savage rifle at the Ross River Post, along with some .22 shells and two of Johnson's guns were a .30-30 Savage rifle and a Winchester .22. Mr. W. W. Douglas, who worked for Northern Traders Limited in Fort McPherson, recalled selling Johnson a 16-gauge single barrel shot-gun and a box of twenty-five shells on July 12, 1931, three days after he arrived at that post.

All the persons who had seen or talked to Arthur Nelson between Ross River Post where he was first seen and McQuesten River where he was last seen were eventually shown facial photos taken of Albert Johnson after death. Most thought it could be the same man, although none could be sure. Johnson was in such an emaciated condition at the time of his death — 65.6–68 kg (145-150 pounds) — that it is explainable that his gaunt features would look somewhat different from the sturdy Nelson of 77 kg (170 pounds).

There was one other question that arose when attempts were made to link Johnson and Nelson and that was whether a man could travel from McQuesten River near Keno — Nelson was last seen there in May 1931 — to Fort McPherson, a distance of some 405 km (250 miles), in just over two months on foot — Johnson first appeared there July 9, 1931. To do so, he would have to cross over the Ogilvie Range. This question was answered by Superintendent Thomas B. Caulkin who commanded the RCMP at Dawson. He said he knew a man who left Mayo on June 28, 1934, went to Fort McPherson and returned to Mayo in the latter part of August 1934, thus doing double the trip in a two-month period.

Over the years since this bizarre affair, the Force has answered numerous inquiries from persons all over the world claiming to be relatives of "The Mad Trapper From Rat River" as he has been described in numerous articles. In each case the RCMP has patiently checked photos and descriptions, and has always had to write back: "We find that . . . is not identical with the man known as Albert Johnson."

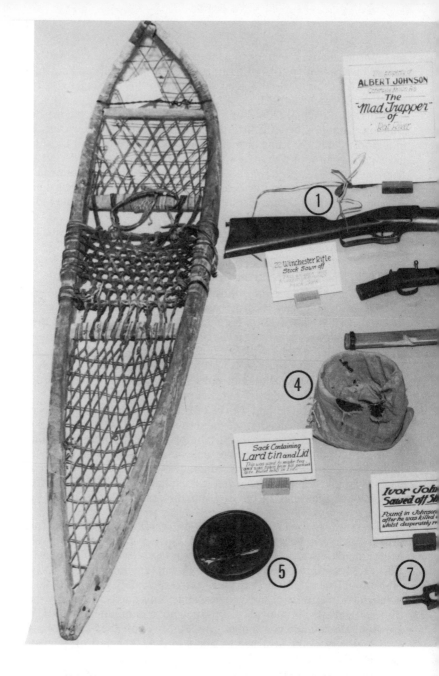

Property of
ALBERT JOHNSON
The "Mad Trapper" of
Rat River

22 Winchester Rifle
Stock Sawn off

Sack Containing
Lard tin and Lid

Ivor Joh...
Sawed off Sh...
Found in Johnson...
after he was killed...
whilst desperately r...

EFFECTS OF ALBERT JOHNSON

1. The .30-30 Savage rifle with which Johnson killed Millen and seriously wounded King and Hersey.

2. Winchester .22 rifle with sawn off stock.

3. Axe with a bullet groove in the handle.

The labels visible in the photograph read:

Savage 30-30 Rifle
This is the Weapon used
By
Johnson
In the Shooting of.
Reg N° 10021 Cst. A.L. King on Dec 31, 1931
Seriously Wounded
Reg N° 9669 Cst. E. Millen on Jan 30 1932
Killed
Staff Sgt. H.F. Hersey, on Feb 17 1932
Royal Canadian Corps of Signal Seriously wounded

Axe
Part of Johnson's Camp
equipment. Note where
Police posse bullet struck
The handle.

Examination Revealed
30-30 Shell
In Hole under Butt Plate

Pocket Compass.
also found in Packsack

4. Lard tin Johnson used for making tea.

5. Bullet-pierced lid of the lard tin.

6. A .30-30 shell concealed behind the butt plate of the Savage rifle.

7. Ivor Johnson sawn-off shotgun.

8. Pocket compass.

9. Snowshoes which weighed ten pounds each.

(All of these items are displayed at the RCMP Museum at Regina, Saskatchewan.)

TRAPPING *the* *of* RAT

THE SENSATIONAL CAPTURE

(As already noted, among those involved in the blizzard-shrouded pursuit of Albert Johnson was World War One fighter ace and famed bush pilot W. R. "Wop" May, DFC. In 1932, in collaboration with H. R. Kincaid, he wrote an account of his experiences which appeared in True Detective Mysteries *and is reprinted courtesy the magazine. The photos are somewhat dark since no archives in Canada seems to have them and they have been reproduced from the original magazine article. It is the first time that they have appeared in a Canadian publication.)*

Canada's Northland was aroused as never before when Sergeant Riddell mushed into Aklavik with the news of Millen's murder. Once again the local radio station, UZK, broadcast Inspector Eames' appeal to trappers and

MAD TRAPPER RIVER
OF ALBERT JOHNSON

The above title and illustration, reprinted from *True Detective Mysteries*, shows supplies being transferred from the Bellanca to a dog team during the Johnson pursuit. The inset photos are of Wop May, left, and Constable Millen.

Indians to join the hunt; and over the moccasin telegraph, UZK's prehistoric cousin, the word was also carried all over the Arctic.

"Get the mad trapper of Rat River!" became the watchword of the North from February 1 onward; and that day saw every man fit to take the trail mushing for Aklavik behind his dog-team.

Meanwhile, at police headquarters, Inspector Eames was marshalling his forces and laying plans for a new campaign against the murderer.

The Inspector was faced by the tremendous handicap that Arctic dwellers, up to that time, had never overcome — the problem of transporting bulky supplies of food, ammunition and dog rations over long distances and through 45-below blizzards. But with a touch of genius Inspector Eames solved that problem in a flash.

He would have an airplane sent in from the "outside" if possible. It would assure ample supplies for his posse without long, heartbreaking marches over the frozen tundra from Aklavik. It would permit both men and dogs to conserve their strength for the primary task of running Johnson down. It would also prove invaluable in scouting the fugitive's position, and speed up communication between Aklavik and other posts lying in the surrounding district.

A plane might also be used to bomb Johnson's stronghold, in the event that aerial bombs were available at Edmonton; and a machine-gun, mounted on the plane, might also be used for an overhead attack.

As a consequence on February 2, I received a wire from "Punch" Dickins, Canadian Airways Superintendent at Edmonton, asking me if it would be possible to fly down to Aklavik and join the Mounted Police in their search. I replied that I was ready to undertake the flight. I received an answering wire from Punch saying he would fly into Fort McMurray, my base, next morning with two Mounted Police officers and a supply of tear-gas bombs.

Next morning, with the thermometer at 35 below, Punch swooped in from Edmonton. I had my engine already running on our 'drome on the Saye River, and we hurriedly transferred the supplies and the tear-gas bombs. Constable Carter, who was going North to replace the murdered Millen, climbed in with me and my air mechanic, Jack Bowen, a veteran of the Arctic. A minute later I had given her the gun and we were soaring down the Athabasca, off on our 2,400-km (1,500-mile) hop to the town of Aklavik.

Flying low in the shelter of the steep banks of the Athabasca, we roared along at 190 km (120 miles) an hour. The weather was fairly good despite the low temperature for the first 160 km (100 miles) of our journey. Thereafter we ran into snowstorms, and by the time we were approaching Fort Smith a blizzard was howling up the river from the Arctic. Since there was no time to be gained by hurrying past Smith and possibly being forced down in the wilderness beyond, I decided to spend the night at the post. We had completed 425 km (265 miles) of the northward hop when we landed in the storm with the shadows of the long Arctic nights creeping in.

Next day, although the weather was threatening and the thermometer way down to 30 below, I decided to hop off. We again sped down river, keeping low in the shelter of the river banks to avoid the stiff north wind. As I feared, we again ran into snow about an hour north of Fort Smith and fifteen minutes later we were ploughing, almost blind, through a howling blizzard. By noon, we had reached Fort Simpson, 740 km (460 miles) down river from Fort Smith, so I landed there and spent the night.

The weather was still pretty bad next morning and the thermometer had dropped another 15 degrees to 45 below. However, we finally decided to start for Fort Norman, 480 km (300 miles) further north. That day was one of the worst that I have ever experienced in the years I have been flying in the Arctic. We bucked snowstorms and gale-force north winds all the way down the river. Near Fort Norman, at 1,200 m (4,000 ft.), the wind had increased to hurricane force. Although at times I had my throttle wide open, we were being blown backward over the ground. Then a blizzard blotted out the earth and left us bumping about up there, completely blind. I guess both Carter and Jack were glad to see the snow under our skis when I eased the Bellanca down to a landing in the storm. I know I was. We had been four hours making the 480-km (300-mile) journey, and our average cruising speed was 190 km (120 miles) an hour.

It was still 45 below zero when we went to our machine next morning and started to dig her clear of the drifts. But the storm had abated, and we took off for Arctic Red River at the junction of the Arctic Red and the Mackenzie Rivers. There I received instructions to meet Inspector Eames' posse at their main camp at the mouth of the Rat and Peel Rivers. We hopped over there from Arctic Red River, but since there wasn't a sign of the posse, I flew on to Aklavik where we spent the night.

Aklavik was storm-swept next morning, a blizzard swirling down from the Arctic on an icy north wind. Again we dug the machine out of the drifts and by 11:35 the storm had abated enough to let us get into the air. I took Doctor Urquhart, Constable Carter, and Jack with me, and flew through snow flurries to Inspector Eames' main camp at the mouth of the Rat and Husky Rivers.

Again I was unable to find their camp but I continued up the Rat to its junction with the Barrier. Suddenly, I saw four men spread out on the snow, creeping up on a clump of bushes on the bank of a creek.

I circled over them trying to spot their objective, but I could see nothing. Finally, they stood up. I learned later that they had been crawling up on a camp where Johnson had spent the night.

I was able to pick up Johnson's trail at this camp. So, flying with our skis almost brushing the snow, I followed his tracks up the Barrier River about 8 km (5 miles). Here the fugitive had circled and come back along his own trail for a distance, as though watching to see if he was followed. There, the fleeing trapper had turned away from the Barrier River, striking westward through a mountain valley toward the range that separated Yukon and the Northwest Territories. His trail disappeared when he came to a snow plain beaten as hard as ice by the scouring winds from the north. I spent half an hour circling over that area trying to pick up his tracks again. But, as the light was failing and I still had to find the posse's camp, I was forced to abandon the search.

I backtracked along Johnson's trail to his old camp. There I picked up the trail of the posse and flew along it to the Mounties' advance camp on the Rat River. I searched for fifteen minutes for a place to land, eventually deciding on a tiny plain between two towering hills. I set the Bellanca down, and I don't mind saying I was mighty proud of that landing. It was a tough spot to get into. In fact one of the greatest handicaps we faced throughout the search would prove to be finding landing grounds in the tangle of hills, box canyons, creeks and rivers. We were working continually over a mighty treacherous country where an engine failure made a crash inevitable, and

A view from 9,145 m (30,000 ft.) of the winding Rat River and general area where Johnson killed Constable Millen.

A constant problem for May during the search was finding a piece of ground flat enough to land on.

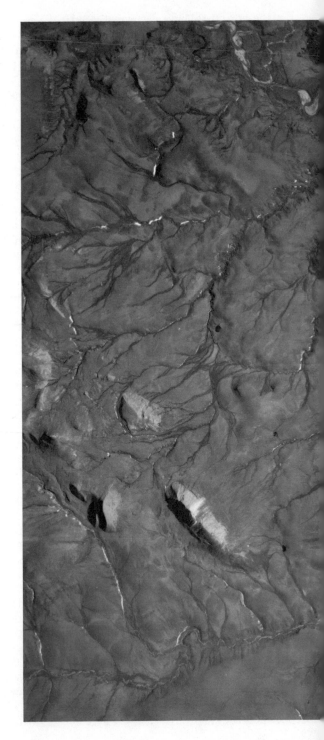

Rat River

MILLEN KILLED HERE o

where the slightest error in judgement, landing or getting off, would have meant a crack-up.

I got into communication with the camp and made arrangements to bring the posse supplies and dog feed from Aklavik. Constable Carter, who had flown in from Edmonton with us, left to join the posse. With Doctor Urquhart and Jack, I flew back to Aklavik for the night.

Next morning (February 8) UZK picked up a message from Inspector

Eames asking me to meet him at the advance camp on Rat River. Jack and I loaded the Bellanca with supplies and dog feed, dug her out of the snow drifts and hopped off for the Rat. The thermometer was down to 45 below, and a flying scud of snow whipping in from the north on a piercing wind froze the marrow of one's bones.

I met the Inspector at the Rat River camp. Here I learned of the terrible difficulties his posse had encountered on their trip from Aklavik.

This photo by Wop May shows the hazardous terrain over which he flew and through which the posse battled in blizzards and sub-zero cold.

Mushing out of Aklavik, the Inspector said they had found the trails buried in 120 cm (4 ft.) of soft snow. Throughout that day, turn by turn, the posse toiled ceaselessly through the drifts, tramping out trail with their snowshoes for the straining dogs. The storm continued to rage all that night and throughout the succeeding four days. Each day found the posse wearily tramping out trail and battling the subzero wind. Throughout that ninety-six hours, their field of vision had been limited to 9–13 m (30–45 ft.) by whirling snow clouds. It required all their trail craft to keep on their course. So slow was their progress, the Inspector said, that they did not reach Johnson's barricade until the following Saturday.

We found the posse encamped in the brush along the Rat River. The men were living in their canvas tents floored with spruce boughs, with small portable stoves to keep them warm and, Arctic fashion, sleeping on caribou skins under eiderdowns. Their tents, when we arrived, were practically buried in the drifting snow.

Included in Inspector Eames' posse at this time were Sergeant Riddell, Sergeant Hersey, and Constable Carter; trappers Noel Verville, Carl Gardlund, Frank Lang, Jack Ethier, Frank Carmichael, Pete Stromberg, and a number of other trappers and Indians. In addition, the Reverend G. Murray, Anglican rector of Aklavik, had mushed out with the Mounties to help in rounding up the mad slayer of Constable Millen.

After discussing plans with Inspector Eames and warning the posse of Johnson's habit of backtracking and watching his own trail, I took Sergeant Riddell, who was familiar with the country, on a flight to search for Johnson's trail.

The light that day was very bad, even for the Arctic, with low–hanging clouds and a gusty wind hinting at a new blizzard. We flew down the Rat River, crossed through a 610–m (2,000–ft.) pass over the mountain range that lay on the Yukon–Northwest Territories boundary, and circled the Yukon country. Although we covered over 240 km (150 miles), we didn't find a trace of Johnson's trail. By the time we got back to the posse's camp, the threatening storm had broken in a flurry of snow. Jack and I loaded Constable Millen's body, frozen as hard as iron, into the Bellanca and I hopped back to Aklavik.

Next day (February 9) one of the worst blizzards that I have ever seen was blowing, making it absolutely impossible for us to leave the ground.

By the following morning the storm had blown itself out, but the temperature was once more down to 45 below. Jack and I, after digging the Bellanca out of the drifts, again took off for the posse's camp, carrying supplies and with Joe Verville, a brother of Noel, as a passenger. When we arrived over the Rat River camp the wind was blowing a gale. Snow, as fine as talcum powder in the extreme cold, was blown 300 m (1,000 ft.) into the air. It was impossible for us to see the ground. I turned back to Aklavik, and flew practically blind down the treacherous, winding Rat River Pass, expecting any moment to bump into one of the snow–covered hills along its course. That was a hair–raising flight, if I ever made one.

We landed at Aklavik at 11 a.m. and waited three hours to see if the gale would moderate with the waning day. At 2 p.m., although a strong wind was still blowing, I decided to try it again. Over the Rat we found conditions worse — if that was possible. I managed, however, to land my supplies at the mouth of the river. I flew from there to Arctic Red, picked up more supplies, and took them back to the Rat. Then, with the posse assured of supplies for a couple of days, we returned to Aklavik after one of the worst flying days in my experience.

During these two days the ground party had been practically storm-bound in their Rat River camp. Some members of the party, though, had taken the trail the second day, but the howling gale and the hurtling snow made it impossible for them to pick up any sign of Johnson's trail.

On February 11 I took off once more from Aklavik with Joe Verville as passenger and a load of supplies, dog feed and ammunition. I swooped in to land on the side-hill where I had been sitting down on my previous visits to the camp and where there had been several feet of hard-pack snow. At the last minute before my skis touched the ground I realized that the gales of the previous two days had scoured the snow practically down to rock. I braced myself for a crash. But the old Bellanca settled down as though there were 6 m (20 ft.) of snow under her skis instead of 4 cm (1½ ins.). I drew a long breath of relief.

Since a bad wind was still whipping across the hills, we hurried the job of unloading supplies. Nevertheless, the wind had again strengthened to a gale before we finished this task and I was compelled to take off hurriedly to save the machine. I flew to Arctic Red River for another load of supplies, landed them at the Rat, and then went back to Aklavik when we found weather conditions made it impossible to search for Johnson's trail.

During this time, members of the ground posse had at last found traces of Johnson's trail further up the Rat. They reported that his tracks wandered in and out of the Divide, sometimes in an apparently aimless manner. At frequent intervals Johnson had backtracked cunningly, taking advantage of the broken country to watch his own trail and ambush pursuers.

But most significant to the trail-wise eyes that were scanning his tracks was the irregular spacing of the snowshoe prints. There was exultation in the voices of the posse as they declared that Johnson's tracks showed that he was starting to weaken under the deadly grind of keeping the trail. He was no longer striding out strongly as he had done in the days when the hunt had been young 80 km (50 miles) further down the Rat.

Next day, in 35-below weather with the wind still blowing frigidly from the north, I flew to the mouth of the Rat for a conference with Inspector Eames and Sergeant Riddell.

"Johnson is undoubtedly heading for the Yukon," Inspector Eames told us. "And, although his latest tracks indicate that he is weakening, he's at least two days ahead of us. He must have been hitting the trail through those two days of blizzard. He may have had a rest since then, of course.

"I think we've got too many men in the field. It's a terrible strain keeping them supplied with food, dog rations and ammunition, and so I'm considering sending some of them home. If we could definitely establish that Johnson's in Yukon, we won't need them anyway, for we can't keep them supplied there."

Eventually, it was decided that Riddell and I should attempt another scouting trip across the Divide into Yukon. We therefore took off, swung up the Rat and again crossed the tortuous, dangerous pass that crossed the Divide at 610 m (2,000 ft.). We flew as low as we possibly could under existing weather conditions, but failed completely to find a trace of the fugitive and returned to Eames' camp.

There, at last, we heard the most welcome news that had come to the posse in many days. Shortly after Riddell and I had started, Constable A.

Above: A camp in the sub-zero weather that was a characteristic of the chase.

Opposite: The posse ready to mush out from one of their wilderness camps. The team in the foreground is driven by Sergeant Riddell, standing behind the sleigh.

May, Mounted Police officer from Old Crow Post in the Yukon, mushed into Inspector Eames' camp to join the hunt. May was accompanied by Frank Jackson, a grey-haired, huge-bodied trader who had been at La Pierre House for years, and who knew that section of Yukon better than any other white man. Another trapper, Frank Hogg, completed May's party.

These three had had no inkling that Johnson was Yukon bound in his flight and the Inspector, who had been hoping that they had brought definite information, was disappointed. But half an hour after they had mushed into camp an Indian, Peter Alexei, also from La Pierre House, came flogging his dog team into camp as though the devil were on his heels.

"Johnson is in Yukon," Alexei shouted to the Inspector as soon as he stopped his dogs. "Some hunters saw his tracks along the Bell River two days ago. Another hunting party passed along there just a few hours earlier, and there wasn't a sign of tracks. They went out from La Pierre House and examined them — and they were Johnson's all right! We found them about a mile below the post!"

Alexei, breathless with excitement, went on to tell the posse that the Indians in the La Pierre House territory were terrorized by the news. They had abandoned their trap lines and fled into the post.

"That's our man, all right!" Inspector Eames said with an air of quiet conviction. "I don't think there's the slightest doubt about it. He's managed to get across the Divide, and he's hitting west into Yukon!"

The Inspector sat silent for a moment, a suggestion of admiration in his eyes. "That man's some musher! Ninety miles in three days — without dogs — and through blizzards! But I think we've got him — at last!"

The Inspector decided to send a ground party over the Divide into Yukon, while he, with other members of the party, would fly west to La Pierre House.

He ordered Sergeant Hersey, Constable May, Frank Hogg, Frank Jackson, Jack Ethier, and Peter Alexei, with two Indian interpreters, to make the passage through the mountains by dog team. The air party included the Inspector, Sergeant Riddell, Carl Gardlund, Jack Bowen and myself.

The ground party took the trail that morning and, about the same time, we flew back to Aklavik to pick up supplies, dog feed and ammunition to be flown into the new search area.

Next morning (February 13) we hopped off for La Pierre House, an ancient trading-post on a loop of the Bell River, necessitating a 160-km (100-mile) flight. Up the Rat we ran into a smother of gale-tossed snow that blotted out the landscape and made our attempt to cross the 2,450-m (8,000-ft.) range of mountains exceptionally hazardous. We struck the wrong pass on our first try and floundered around, almost blind with jagged peaks sticking up under our wing tips.

I was sweating plenty under my parka, and it wasn't with the heat, either, when we finally found the right pass and came down out of the smother on the Yukon side. We found a heavy snowstorm in progress at La Pierre House. After we landed I was compelled to taxi the Bellanca up and down for half an hour to make a runway so I could get off again.

A ground party was sent from La Pierre House to examine the tracks south of there. They returned that night and reported that they were unquestionably Johnson's, but that they appeared to be at least four days' old. Although we received that information in a rather crestfallen manner, it compelled the admission that this man Johnson was a superman on the trail. It seemed almost incredible that a man without dogs could make such time under such terrible trail conditions.

Early next day (February 14) I again took off to follow Johnson's trail. I picked up his tracks without difficulty in the deep snow at La Pierre House and followed them easily around the looping bend of the Bell River for over 40 km (25 miles). But where the Eagle River flowed into the Bell thousands of caribou had left a wide, hard-packed trail on the river bottom.

Here Johnson had discarded his snowshoes. His trail had vanished once more!

I cast about in wide circles to try to pick up his tracks again, but the fugitive, sticking cunningly to the caribou trail, had covered his retreat. So I flew back to La Pierre House. On the way I saw where the posse could gain a tremendous advantage by cutting across country. It was 40 km (25 miles) following the Bell River loop along Johnson's trail, but by taking the overland route, the posse could accomplish the distance to the mouth of the Eagle River in less than half that distance.

I recommended this route to Inspector Eames when I landed back at La Pierre House. He immediately adopted my suggestion. Right there the posse gained at least three days on their quarry.

I found Inspector Eames had been investigating Johnson's trail from the ground. South of La Pierre House, evidently warned of the proximity of the post by howling dogs, the fugitive had made a wide detour, swinging back to the Bell River west of the trading center. He camped one night less than a mile west of the post. Farther west still, the ground party discovered

The only way that mechanic Jack Bowen and Wop May could service the Bellanca in the frigid weather was by laboriously covering the engine with a tent.

The photo opposite shows the skis that enabled the plane to successfully challenge the deep, powdery snow.

where Johnson had laid a fire. Then something, possibly the howling of dogs, frightened him and he had dashed off again on his mad westward trek. Still farther west, the pursuers found Johnson's snowshoe track was again wobbling pitifully, indicating that he was once more on the verge of exhaustion. The heavy snows and the unremitting exertion were cutting into even his iron constitution.

The Inspector informed me that supplies at La Pierre House were practically exhausted. Food especially was short since the Indians who had flocked into the post on the word that the "mad trapper" was in their midst had consumed practically everything. I decided to fly back to Aklavik, pick up supplies there, and gas and oil for my machine.

But once again I encountered trouble in that treacherous 610-m (2,000-ft.) pass through the mountains. A blinding snowstorm was whooping through the pass when Jack and I arrived. Once again we floundered around among those jagged peaks for a hair-raising quarter of an hour before I gave up and went back to La Pierre House.

About midnight, the ground party which mushed over the Divide staggered into the post. Men and dogs were completely worn out by their battle with deep snow, lashing gales, and the fierce cold of high altitudes. They lay like dead men that night, asleep almost before they had crawled under their eiderdowns.

Next morning (February 15) when they awoke, snow was still falling heavily and a frigid wind still blowing from the north. But they hitched up their whining dogs and flogged them into the storm, bound by the overland

A common occurrence during the northland pursuit — digging the plane out of a heavy snowfall.

route for Eagle River where Johnson's trail had disappeared in the maze of caribou tracks. Inspector Eames and Sergeant Riddell again took the trail with them, making a party of eleven. They included Constable May, Sergeant Hersey, Verville, Gardlund, Ethier, Jackson, Alexei, and two Indian interpreters.

I thought, as I watched that party tramp stolidly out into the whirling snow that morning, that I had never seen a more determined body of men. The discovery of Johnson's faltering tracks had spurred them to a dogged resolve that the fugitive would henceforth get no rest — no chance to recoup his failing strength. I wouldn't have wanted those men, in their frame of mind, on my trail!

By noon the storm had cleared sufficiently to allow Jack and me to start for Aklavik. We spent three hours digging the old Bellanca out of the snowdrift and soared away to try our luck again with the pass. This time we had no difficulty, and arrived back at La Pierre House that afternoon heavily laden with supplies, ammunition, gas and oil.

Next day, the weather was again completely impossible. Throughout the brief hours of daylight the snow fell so thickly that it was impossible to see for more than a few yards. We sat helplessly in La Pierre House and wondered if Johnson was making another 32-km (20-mile) gain on us. We also felt plenty sorry for men and dogs who were out on the trail in such a storm.

February 17 dawned in a grey blanket of fog and snow, but by 10:30 the fog had lifted enough to give some semblance of visibility. Jack and I,

shovelling like slaves, dug the Bellanca out of the night's accumulation of snow, got her running and then swung off northward for Eagle River.

Since I arranged with Sergeant Riddell for him to place arrows along his trail, Jack and I had no difficulty in following Eames' posse. We cut across the wide-swinging loop of the Bell on their track and in a few minutes sighted the Eagle River.

This stream, winding like a snake through precipitous banks, flowed down from a range of hills southwest of the Bell, and joined the latter river about 50 km (30 miles) west of La Pierre House.

We were droning along about 190 km (120 miles) an hour when I glanced down to the river bottom. I saw a black speck on the ice in the center of the stream. Puzzled, I stared at it for a second. Then perhaps 360 m (1,200 ft.) south of the lone speck I noticed half a dozen other specks spread out at the foot of the steep eastern bank of the river. A movement on the high western bank directed my attention to two more specks standing out clearly against the dead white of the snow background.

A glinting flash caught my eye near the east bank.

Then, with a fierce thrill, the significance of the scene struck me. That lone black speck in the center of the river was Johnson — the mad trapper! The other specks were the posse crouched along the river bank in its cover. And that glinting flash was the flame of a rifle.

Johnson, at last, had been brought to bay on the river ice. He was again matching his rifle against the rifles of Eames' command.

Would they "get him" this time? Or would his luck still hold? And would we go on chasing him up and down through these hills, up and down these rivers through blizzards and cold and the dingy half-light of Arctic days?

My mind seething with these thoughts, I cut my motor and glided down above the river bottom. Above the keening of the wind around the Bellanca's skin I could hear the crackle of the rifles below. Watching with fascinated eyes, I also could now catch the flash of the weapons and see the snow dance under the impact of the bullets.

As I swept over Johnson, scarcely 15 m (50 ft.) above him, I could see where he had dug himself a shallow lair in the hard-packed snow of the river bottom, and tossed his pack on the snow in front of him to hide his movements from his foes.

I heard his rifle crack as I opened the throttle and flew south in a wide circle. We came roaring back down the river. Once again I peered down at Johnson in his snow trench as we raced overhead. Then, as I passed over the posse, I saw a figure lying on a bed-roll near the west bank. I realized, with a sick feeling, that one of our party had been hit.

Who was it? And was he dead?

Busy with these torturing thoughts I circled and came back upriver, passing over the posse and Johnson. As I flew over the fugitive's lair it appeared to me that he was lying in an unnatural position. When I came back the next time, I nosed the Bellanca down until our skis were tickling the snow on the river bottom. Johnson, I could plainly see as I flashed past, was lying face down in the snow, his right arm outflung, grasping his rifle.

There is something about the way a dead man lies that is unmistakable. I knew, as I looked at Johnson, that he was dead. The Mounties had "got their man." The chase was over!

I rocked the Bellanca back and forth on her wing-tips to signal Johnson's death to the posse. Then I landed on the river bottom and taxied over to where I had seen the man on the bed-roll.

"Who's hit?" I called as Jack and I clambered out of the machine. Sergeant Riddell, who was bending over the wounded man, answered: "Sergeant Hersey."

"Badly?" I asked.

"I'm afraid so." Sergeant Riddell's face was grave for Hersey was his particular pal. "He's wounded in the left knee, and it may have gone up into his stomach."

I considered a moment, and then said: "Get him fixed up as well as you can and I'll fly him to hospital at Aklavik."

Sergeant Riddell started to prepare Hersey for the trip, and I strolled up the river toward Johnson's lair where members of the posse were staring at the dead man. As I joined the crowd, Verville turned to me and said: "Just look at his face, Wop. Did you ever see anything like it?"

I stepped around to get a look at Johnson's face. He was lying face down on the river. As I stooped over and saw him, I got the worst shock I think I've ever had.

Johnson's lips were curled from his teeth in the most terrible sneer I've ever seen on a man's face. The parchment-like skin over his cheek bones was distorted by it, while his teeth glistened like an animal's through his days'-old bristle of beard. It was the most awful grimace of hate I'll ever see — the hard boiled, bitter hate of a man who knows he's trapped at last, and who has determined to take as many enemies as he can with him.

After that sneer, I couldn't feel sorry for this man who lay dead in front of me. Instead, I was glad that he was dead. The world seemed a better place with him out of it.

I sneaked another look at that sneer. Then, cold with aversion, half sick, I turned away. I knew that the other members of the posse felt the same way as I did as we walked away from Johnson's body. At the Bellanca where Riddell was preparing Hersey for the flight to hospital, I heard the story of Johnson's last stand as the posse had seen it from the ground.

Early that morning, they told me, they had broken camp near the mouth of the Eagle River and started upstream along the caribou trail. Inspector Eames, armed only with a revolver, had been the first to mush out along the frozen river behind his dogs and, during the first hour and a half, had led the posse.

Then, however, Hersey overtook the Inspector and forged into the lead. The fact that Hersey's dogs were slightly faster than the Inspector's was the lucky circumstance that saved Eames' life. For Eames, armed only with a revolver, would have been no match for Johnson's deadly rifle, although the Inspector is one of the best revolver shots in the Arctic.

Hersey sighted Johnson first as he rounded a bend in the river. The fugitive was frenziedly trying to scramble up the steep, ice-crusted river bank and take cover in the brush. Johnson finally abandoned his attempt and flung himself down facing Hersey.

The photo above, taken by Wop May, shows Johnson dead on the ice, and part of the plane's wing and air speed indicator.

The Eagle River from 9,145 m (30,000 ft.), showing the bend where the posse caught up to Johnson.

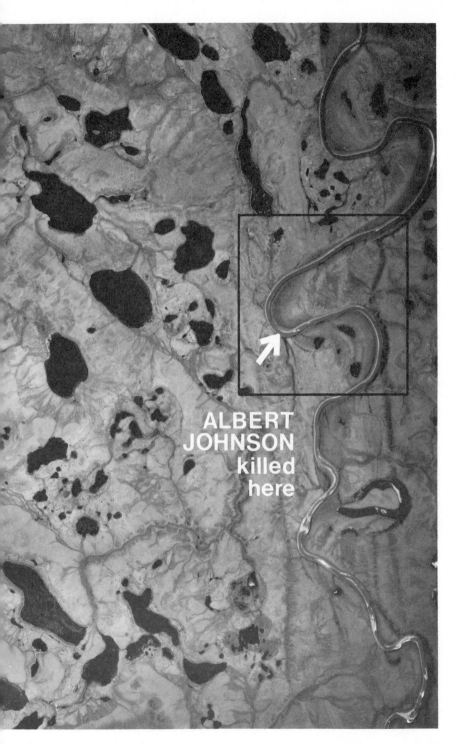

ALBERT
JOHNSON
killed
here

The Sergeant seized his rifle from the sleigh, and dashed toward the center of the river bottom to get a better view of the fugitive. Verville, in the meantime, had joined Hersey and they took up positions a short distance apart. Hersey was kneeling on one knee sighting his rifle, calm and unflustered, when Johnson hit him. Verville, wincing, saw the Sergeant topple over and collapse on the ice.

The other members of the party — Sergeant Riddell, Constable May, Gardlund, Jackson, Ethier, Alexei and the two Indians — had heard the rifle shots. They came dashing around the bend in the river, dog-whips cracking as they sped along the trail, eager to get into the battle.

Johnson, seeing these reinforcements, instantly decided upon flight. He sprang up and started at a shambling gallop back along his trail. Behind him, the members of the posse raced to the river bank.

One by one, the rifles of the party roared into action. Under the volley Johnson suddenly staggered and then toppled to the ice. Members of the posse saw him dig himself frantically out of sight in the hard-packed snow then toss his bed-roll in front of him as a shield.

Taking advantage of the cover along the river bank, the posse worked its way closer to the fugitive. Around the bed-roll the snow danced as rifle bullets ripped their way through it.

Johnson's blazing rifle answered shot for shot, and the crackle of his bullets kept the posse crouching behind their cover.

It was at this stage of the battle that Frank Jackson, the veteran La Pierre trader, gave a demonstration of cool courage that was to be talked about in the Northland for many months.

"I'm out of ammunition, boys!" Jackson yelled to his posse mates. "I'll range for you."

With these words, Jackson heaved his huge body out from behind a bush where he had been lying and calmly walked up the river bank. From this point of vantage, looking down on Johnson's position, he called out ranging directions.

"A little high — a little low — a little to the right!" Jackson shouted to the posse as their rifles crashed in the river canyon below him. Jackson was still directing their fire, as though he was on a rifle range, when I finally swooped down over Johnson's trench and signalled that he was dead.

By this time, the members of the posse had picked up Johnson's body and his bullet-riddled bed-roll and loaded them upon Verville's sleigh for the trip back to La Pierre House. There followed the maddest battle with a husky team that I have ever seen. Verville's dogs, terrified by the grim burden lashed on their sleigh, howled dismally and fought against taking the trail. But Joe tore into them with butt and lash and, as I turned away to start for Aklavik with Hersey, we could hear Verville's dogs howling a death march down the frozen river. It was one of the weirdest sights I had ever seen in the North.

Sergeant Riddell, in the meantime, had prepared Hersey as best he could for the flight. The wounded officer was not bleeding much from his wound and was fully conscious. But it was a difficult task getting him into the Bellanca and in a comfortable position. Finally, Jack Bowen decided he could carry him best on his knee. I took Sergeant Riddell along with us in case we should have a forced landing since it was impossible for Jack to get out of the machine with Hersey on his knee.

With four of us in the Bellanca's cabin, I gave her the gun and we were off on our 200-km (125-mile) flight to Aklavik.

As I climbed out of the crooked Eagle River and hit across country for the Bell, I wondered what sort of weather I would find in that treacherous pass through the mountains. I wasn't long in finding out.

As I climbed through the hills, the Bellanca was nosing through thick fog. When we finally hit the pass at 610 m (2,000 ft.) I couldn't see both sides of the canyon at once. But there wasn't to be any turning back this trip — Hersey's life might pay the forfeit. I shut my teeth and let the old Bellanca drone along, and hedge-hopped through. More than once I thought we were sunk when a jagged peak leaped at us through the murk, and whistled past within a few inches of our wing-tip.

But we got through. Fifty minutes from the time of taking off from the Eagle River we had Hersey in hospital at Aklavik and Doctor Urquhart was cutting his parka off.

The Doctor found Hersey gravely wounded. Johnson's bullet had struck him in the left elbow, ploughed through his left knee, drilled his arm near the armpit, and then ripped through his body, piercing both lungs in its passage. The bullet was found just under the skin in the Sergeant's back.

Doctor Urquhart's face was grim when he had completed his examination of Hersey, and stopped the hemorrhages from the lungs.

"He's in a very serious condition — very," the Doctor told us. "But we may pull him through. Another half hour would have finished him. It wouldn't have taken those hemorrhages long."

I felt repaid for that blind flight through the pass, although it had been nip and tuck in more ways than one.

We stayed in Aklavik that night and Jack and I hopped off again next morning to once again challenge the stormy mountain pass. This time, though, we sailed through without difficulty and landed at La Pierre House in fairly good weather.

I learned further details there from Inspector Eames of the final phases of the hunt.

Johnson, it had been learned, had crossed the Divide over the highest peak — over 2,400 m (8,000 ft.). Apparently he had been afraid to keep to the pass. That trip over the mountains must have been one long agony for him. Since there wasn't a scrap of firewood available, the fugitive must have spent at least one night in that high altitude without a fire.

We marvelled anew at the tremendous vitality this man must have possessed and the indomitable will power he had shown in tackling the mountains. Few people in the Arctic cross those mountains in the winter-time, even with dogs and plenty of supplies, unless they are compelled to.

The police had learned that Johnson was wounded many times in his last stand. The first bullet which had struck him as he was fleeing from the posse hit his hip pocket where he was carrying part of his ammunition. This ammunition had exploded with the impact, tearing a huge wound in his hip. All the other wounds were in his legs, back and shoulders. The bullet which ended the fugitive's grim life had passed through the small of his back, severing his spine.

Johnson, the police discovered, had been in terrible physical condition at the end. His feet, legs and both hands were frozen, probably during that night when he had been caught without a fire in the high border mountains. He was thin to the point of emaciation. He had a lard tin for making tea but no cooking utensils. The only bit of food that he had carried was a squirrel which he had evidently shot just a short time before he encountered the posse.

The fugitive had been a walking arsenal. He was armed with a .30–30 Savage rifle, the weapon which had laid three men low in the course of his seven weeks' battle with the law. He had fired every round in it during the last battle, and had been in the act of re–loading when a bullet ended his life.

In addition, Johnson carried a .22 caliber rifle and the 16-gauge shotgun that he bought the previous fall in Fort McPherson.

The shotgun was the most amazing weapon seen in the Arctic Circle. It had been sawed off within a few inches of the stock.

"A sawed-off shotgun in the Arctic," Inspector Eames commented, "that's a weapon that has never been known before here in the North. It's the weapon that gangsters and murderers use in the big cities in the South. What use could a weapon like that be to a trapper? And where would a trapper — especially a 'bushed' trapper — learn to saw off a shotgun?"

I, too, pondered these questions for a long time. And I shuddered as I

Dr. J. W. Urquhart, second from right with hand in pocket, saved the lives of both Constable King and Sergeant Hersey. Others in the photo include, from left, Corporal R. W. Wild, Mrs. Urquhart, Inspector Eames and Constable A. Milvin.

thought of what might have happened if the posse had met this murderous weapon at close range.

Johnson had been plentifully supplied with ammunition, too. In his pocket when his body was searched at La Pierre House the police found between thirty and forty rounds of .30-30 caliber rifle cartridges. All were the explosive type used for hunting big game — particularly deadly in their action. In addition, Johnson carried between fifty and sixty rounds of .22 ammunition together with a few shells for the sawed-off shotgun. The contents of his pockets amazed the police when they turned them out.

On him Johnson had over $2,500 in Canadian and United States currency — a fortune in cash for the Arctic, where most trappers conduct their transactions on trading certificates of the posts with which they do their business. That wasn't the only surprise, either!

A small quantity of gold dust was found in a leather poke, and the police also discovered two gold bridges, presumably from a man's mouth. And — a most sinister circumstance — neither of those bridges came from Johnson's mouth. Who, the police asked, was this man who carried in the Arctic gold bridges ripped from the mouths of other men?

An ordinary, open-blade razor, an axe, and a pocket compass, in addition to his bullet-riddled bed-roll, completed the equipment with which Johnson had been keeping the trail in the last days of the chase. Police believed that the fleeing trapper had carried cooking utensils with him at the start of his flight, but had probably discarded them as he weakened under the strain of the tremendous pace.

The examination of Johnson's belongings revealed another strange trait — everything was wrapped in cloth. His money, divided into a number of small rolls, was stowed away in every pocket. Each of these small rolls was painstakingly wrapped in cloth. His razor and the gold bridges were similarly done up before being stowed in his capacious pockets.

An examination of Johnson's rifle revealed yet another grim bit of evidence that the fugitive had been determined not to come alive into the hands of the police. A loose butt plate on the weapon stirred the officers' curiosity and they removed it. There, cunningly fitted into a niche bored in the wood of the stock, they found a single round of ammunition, carefully wrapped in cloth.

That round, Johnson had unquestionably saved for himself — if the worst came.

There was not a scrap of paper in Johnson's pockets — not a line of writing that might have aided the police in backtracking along his sinister trail through the Territories and Yukon. This circumstance, too, inclined the police to the theory that Johnson was not the simple "bushed" trapper that he had purported to be.

It was at La Pierre House, too, that I learned of the circumstances which had turned Johnson back on his Eagle River trail and finally brought about the last battle with the avenging posse. We had been inclined the previous day to the theory that the fugitive had once more backtracked to protect himself; thus fallen a victim to his own cunning.

But Constable May, the officer from Old Crow, followed Johnson's trail up the Eagle River after the fight. He found, at numerous places, indications that Johnson had mounted the steep river bank to watch his trail. Where he finally turned back, the fleeing man had climbed a tree to scan the river behind him.

My theory is that Johnson, while up this tree, caught sight of the dog teams coming up the river. But, confused by the windings of the stream, Johnson came to the conclusion that the posse was ahead of him instead of behind him. As a consequence, he came straight back to meet them. Only a man who has flown over the Eagle River and seen its maze of windings and turnings from the air could appreciate how easy it would have been to make this mistake. But it is my belief that that's exactly what happened.

Our discussion of the previous day's battle over, Inspector Eames informed me that he would fly back to Aklavik that day, taking Johnson's body and kit with him. Jack and I loaded Johnson's body, his face still distorted in that horrible sneer, into the Bellanca and hopped off for Aklavik. Our return flight was made without incident, and soon we were back at the police post and where the Inspector fingerprinted the dead man. That proved to be a horrible task, too, for Johnson's body was frozen hard as iron and his hands clamped like claws as he had died clutching his rifle.

That horrible sneer was still on Johnson's face the last time I saw him. I suppose they buried him that way. He'll never change. The Arctic cold will keep that sneer unchanged throughout the centuries.

Johnson, as I saw him, was about 178 cm (5 ft. 9 in.) tall. He had exceptionally long arms, and very narrow hips for a man with his chest measurement. His ears, very prominent, were slightly deformed. His hair was far back on his forehead and he had a pug nose with large flaring nostrils.

Next day (February 22) as there was a shortage of supplies at Aklavik, I flew to Arctic Red River, at the junction of the Arctic Red and the Mackenzie, and brought back a load. The following day, my task completed in the North, I left for Fort McMurray. We brought Constable King, who had recovered from his wound sufficiently to go "outside," and Constable Millen's body with us. I was held up for one day by a storm at Fort Simpson on our trip out, and landed at our aerodrome on the river on February 24. It was three weeks to the day since we had left for the North.

I thought then that the end had been written to the Johnson case. But Johnson, his horrible sneer hidden in his grave at Aklavik, was fated still to provide the police with a puzzle. Today he is still as great a mystery as he was the day that he came floating down the Peel River on his log raft.

Early in the chase, when newspapers were blazoning the story of the Rat River hunt across North America, a prairie farmer "recognized" Johnson as an Albert Johnson whom he had known, and who was believed to be trapping in the North. Pictures of this Albert Johnson were reproduced in newspapers throughout the world, labelled as the desperate trapper of the Rat. Police and public, for the moment, were satisfied with that identification.

Then, one day, this Albert Johnson walked into the editorial offices of one of the Western Canadian newspapers which had used his picture, informed the perspiring editor that he was not the "mad trapper," and that he was considering an action for damages against the publishers.

So the police were confronted once more with the puzzling question: Who was this man who, under the name of Albert Johnson, lay in a grave at Aklavik? Dead and buried, the mad trapper brought about a new hunt throughout North America as police officers, working with the prints of his frozen fingers, sought the answer to the puzzle.

Shortly after I returned from Aklavik I got the thrill of my life when I picked up a copy of *True Detective Mysteries* and started to read the stories. I came to one, written by Luke S. May, Seattle criminologist, on his chase through the Craters of the Moon in Idaho on a hunt for Coyote Bill. He was wanted for a hold-up and the murder of a man who was superintendent of an irrigation company in Idaho state. Staring at me from one of the pages was a picture of Coyote Bill.

I gazed at it for a moment, puzzled. Where, I thought, had I seen that face before? It certainly was familiar. Then there crashed back into my mind another face — a face contorted by a hideous sneer as it lay behind a bullet-riddled bed-roll on the ice floor of the Eagle River. The resemblance was striking — and I'm almost certain that Albert Johnson, the mad trapper of Rat River, will prove to be Coyote Bill, the man whom Luke May pursued through the far-off Craters of the Moon in Idaho, and finally was forced to abandon the search.

As I read Mr. May's story, the resemblance between the two men became even more convincing. The Coyote Bill mentioned in his story was a trailsman skilled in every trick of the open spaces. He was a man of iron constitution, and he was reputed to be a deadly shot. Coyote Bill, too, had been a trapper in Idaho and Washington and, when his trail vanished in that state, it was believed that he had fled to Yukon, Alaska or the Canadian North.

Johnson, as we had known our "mad trapper," undoubtedly came from Yukon. Mounted Police now believe that he came down the Yukon River and along the Tatonduk, a tributary that stretches eastward and whose headwaters rise just west of the divide where the Peel and the Porcupine Rivers originate. There isn't the slightest question that Johnson had intended to go down the Porcupine, and thus penetrate the wild, inaccessible, sparsely-settled region in North Yukon where a man could live for years, alone and unrecognized.

What better haven could a man of Coyote Bill's type have desired — a trapper fleeing from civilization with a murder charge hanging over his head? And the description and characteristics — they fitted at every point!

But Fate — a Fate which Johnson cursed bitterly, you will recall, when he learned he was on the wrong stream — betrayed him into launching his raft on the Peel, instead of the Porcupine. This mistake was one which any man might have made, especially if he was unfamiliar with the country. A glance at the map will show that the Porcupine and Peel rise close to each other. As a result, instead of floating down the Porcupine into the absolute wilderness, Johnson came instead to the comparatively thickly settled district around Fort McPherson and the Rat River. This was country where trappers and Indians were numerous, and where the Mounted Police, deadly foes of lawbreakers, maintained several posts and kept in close touch by radio with far-off civilization.

This theory also explains, I believe, the mystery of that fortress cabin which Johnson built in his clearing on the Rat River, and which puzzled the police. It would explain the back-breaking toil which Johnson had undertaken to sink the floor below ground level, and it would explain the double-logged wall and the cunningly placed loopholes that commanded the clearing. Johnson was building, not a simple trapper's cabin, but a fortress from which he could defy the police — if it became necessary.

I believe, too, this theory explains Johnson's attitude toward friendly wilderness visitors who dropped into his camp on the Peel and his cabin on the Rat, only to be ordered brusquely, at the point of a gun to "keep a-goin'." Johnson, if he was Coyote Bill, wouldn't want inquisitive trappers and Indians prying into his secrets.

It explains, I think, the lies which Johnson told Constable Millen on their first encounter in the autumn of 1931 in Fort McPherson, and his growled reply to the Mountie: "I don't want to have anything to do with the police — there's always trouble when they're around."

Johnson, a simple trapper, had no cause to fear the police. But Coyote Bill, with his picture and description and fingerprints on file with these self-same Mounties, would be very chary of meeting any police officers.

Now, if Johnson were Coyote Bill, with a murder on his conscience and a police officer hammering on his fortress door, what was more natural than to fire a treacherous shot through the door, as Johnson fired at Constable King? He would be desperate, cornered and ready to fight for his life — as Johnson obviously was.

There wasn't a single logical reason to explain Johnson's attack on Constable King. Up to the time that he fired that shot, Johnson had no reason to fear the police. The only reason that has ever been advanced for that murderous attack was that he was "bushed" — Arctic crazy. From my experiences in that chase, I'm convinced Johnson was anything but a lunatic.

Finally, I believe Johnson's identification as Coyote Bill would solve the puzzle of the sawed-off shotgun, whose possession by the Rat River fugitive puzzled Inspector Eames. No Arctic trapper, "bushed" as Johnson was supposed to have been from years of loneliness in the North, would have thought of constructing such a murderous weapon. But Coyote Bill, crony of crooks in the underworld, would have been familiar with this deadly thugs' weapon. He would have realized only too thoroughly its vicious advantages in a desperate battle at close range.

I'm pretty nearly certain in my own mind that Johnson, the mad trapper of the Rat River whom justice overtook on the icy bottom of the Eagle River, will prove to be Coyote Bill, the Idaho murderer who outfooted retribution in his dash through the Craters of the Moon.

Time — and the prints of Johnson's frozen fingers — will eventually prove whether I am right.

(Editor's Note: Despite Wop May's web of strong circumstantial evidence linking Coyote Bill to Albert Johnson, the fingerprints did not match.

Police still do not have an answer to the question: Who was the Mad Trapper of Rat River?)

Since the shoot-out in 1932, magazine and newspaper articles, books, a television program and a movie have kept the saga of Albert Johnson before the public. Some of the authors produced accurate accounts, others relied on a vivid imagination. "Inaccurate and ridiculous" was the way Earl Hersey summed up one book. Hersey's opinion of the book is equally applicable to a Hollywood movie, Death Hunt. *The production portrayed Albert Johnson as a superhero instead of a cold-blooded killer and was widely criticized as a "brutal distortion of Canadian history." Two of those most maligned were Corporal Millen and W.R. "Wop" May. Instead of a dedicated policeman who sacrificed his life, Millen is shown as an alcoholic putting in time until retirement. May is equally slandered. He becomes not the pilot who risked his life flying out the gravely wounded Hersey but a bounty hunter who machine guns an RCMP posse tracking Johnson and kills himself by flying into a cliff. In reality, May was a World War One fighter ace who became a legendary bush pilot, famed for his*

Wings over the Wilderness

"Capt. 'Wop' May, OBE, DFC, is one of Canada's most famous airmen but his name would never have been featured in the newspaper headlines if the Goddess of Luck hadn't smiled on him brightly at the very outset of his career as an aviator," newspaperman Jim Coleman summarized in an article in the *Edmonton Bulletin* in 1935 after interviewing May.

The incident which Coleman referred to occurred in 1918 during May's first patrol over the Western Front when he was eighteen. At the time the

Above: The Avro Avian plane on the ice at Peace River Crossing during the 1929 mercy flight. The sternwheelers plied the Peace River for decades, supplying Fort McMurray and other river communities.

Opposite: W.R. May as a lieutenant in the Royal Flying Corps in England in 1917. He shot down his first German plane when he was 18. His nickname, Wop, was born when a young cousin persistently called him "Woppie" while trying to pronounce Wilfred, his first name.

most feared German fighter pilot was Baron Manfred von Richthofen who had shot down eighty planes, killing eighty-seven pilots and crew members. Richthofen was commander of an elite German fighter group nicknamed "The Flying Circus" by Allied pilots because each plane was painted a different color. As Richthofen's was bright red, he became known as the "Red Baron." In the air his favorite technique was to keep on the fringe of a dog fight then chase any planes that were crippled. But even when after cripples, he had an unbroken rule — never cross enemy lines. One morning, however, the Baron broke his rule. In his interview with 'Wop' May, Coleman reported the consequences:

"Eleven years ago this week Baron Manfred Richthofen, master of the famous 'Flying Circus' crashed behind the allied lines at Vaux-sur-Somme, his heart pierced by a bullet from the machine gun of Captain Roy Brown, a former Edmonton boy. That bullet saved the life of Captain 'Wop' May who was at the mercy of the Red Baron, both his guns being jammed.

"The story is one of the most dramatic in the war history of the Royal Flying Corps. Yet when May, after much coaxing, tells it, it sounds like nothing more than a mere bit of routine work.

"On the morning on April 21, 1918, Captain Roy Brown with his squadron of eleven planes, roared up from their base at Bertangles and headed toward Hunland. It was 'Wop' May's first flight into enemy territory and his instructions from Captain Brown were definite. It was the rule of the Corps that a flier on his first trip across the lines must not go into a 'dog fight'. He must hang on the outside and observe how the veterans handled their machines.

"Just as Brown's squadron droned over Corbie on the Somme, Baron Richthofen and his Flying Circus of 30 machines were sighted heading for the Allied lines. Although the British squadron was outnumbered almost three to one, Captain Brown gave the signal to attack. The Germans saw their opponents rushing toward them and came to meet the attack.

"With forty motors and eighty machine guns roaring, the two squadrons went into a dog fight, darting, spinning and writhing high above the trenches from which war-weary infantry watched.

"Following his instructions, 'Wop' May hung above the fight, itching to hurl himself into the uneven battle. As he hovered, a German machine passed underneath. The temptation was too great. May dropped on the Hun like an eagle. Almost in the twinkling of an eye 'Wop' found himself in the midst of the dog fight.

"Rushing straight at the Edmonton boy came one of the Flying Circus, his guns spitting steady streams of lead. Ducking his head, May opened up with his guns trained on the nose of the German machine. The bullets of the German were missing the top of May's wings by a scant few inches. Closer and closer the two machines rushed, and then just when it appeared they were going to meet head on, the Edmonton man slipped under his opponent. May's marksmanship told. The German slumped in his seat and his machine shot earthward with a shriek.

"British and Germans were so intermingled in the dog fight that it was almost impossible to distinguish friend or foe. May accordingly went into a close vertical turn with his guns both going full blast, spraying the enemy planes that swarmed around him like bees. 'Wop's' guns were air cooled and with the terrific heat of continuous firing both stopped.

"May was helpless with both guns stuck and accordingly broke from the dog fight and headed back for his base. Hovering on the outskirt of the battle, waiting for cripples to add to his record of 80 Allied machines, Baron Richthofen dropped on the Edmonton boy. Turning his head as the shower of German bullets whined past him, May saw the bright red machine of Richthofen on his tail. With his throttle wide open 'Wop' shot downward towards the lines, twisting and turning to dodge the fire to which he could not reply. At the height of not more than 150 feet the two machines shot over the lines from which there came a hail of rifle and machine gun fire, some of the bullets piercing the wings of the British machine.

"The Red Baron was not more than twenty-five yards behind his quarry. He had never ventured behind the Allied lines before, but this time he was so enraged at being unable to get the darting cripple that he threw caution to the winds and prepared to make his kill. This time he would not miss. He was so close that it was impossible to miss.

"May turned his head, prepared to make a last effort to dodge the red scourge. Richthofen's face was set in a grin as he trained his gun directly on 'Wop's' back. Then Brown suddenly burst into view, above and behind Richthofen. The same instant his guns cracked. The German's grin changed to a twisted grimace of pain. He straightened in his seat for a fleeting instant, and then slumped forward. One of Brown's bullets had passed through his heart. Out of control, his plane made only a three-quarter spin, so close was it to the ground, and crumpled up into a heap with a crash.

"The Red Baron had at last met the fate he had meted out so often to so many others.

" 'It was only the fact that I was a green flier that saved me,' explained May. 'If I had been an experienced man, Richthofen would have been able to figure out what I would do next and he would have got me.'

"A few minutes later Brown's entire squadron returned to their base without a man so much as scratched. They had met a squadron three times their number and downed three machines. Lieutenant McKenzie, now of New York, getting the third machine."

May was later wounded while strafing German trenches and when the war ended had shot down thirteen planes and won the Distinguished Flying Cross.

When he returned to Edmonton in 1919 he founded May Airlines with his brother, Court, bought a small biplane called the "City of Edmonton" and set out to earn a living. At the time people had virtually no faith in aircraft and the pilot's main source of income was from "barnstorming" — following fairs and similar events, doing aerial acrobatics then landing in the nearest field or river bar and taking people up for rides. As May noted: "A man or woman who had been up in an airplane had sufficient conversation material to last for weeks. We used to get about $15.00 for a five-minute flight, and the customers all seemed happy to pay that price."

"There were no flying fields anywhere. You just picked out a place from the air and if it didn't turn out to be what you thought it was, it was just too bad. I always had good luck in landing, however."

An example of this luck occurred when May was returning to Edmonton with mechanic Pete Derbyshire after a barnstorming tour of the Peace River Country. As May later recounted in an article in the *Edmonton Bulletin:*

"We took off from Grande Prairie and were flying along fine when the radiator developed a leak. The engine started to heat up and I knew we couldn't go on for long like that. Finally the motor became so hot it burned out a hose connection. I knew I had to come down, so I looked over the terrain below. It's a beautiful country in the summer time, but dynamite for a forced landing.

"Finally I spotted a little meadow two or three miles from the Athabasca river, 25 miles west of Whitecourt. We landed all right, but the motor was in pretty bad shape. There we were, in a wild bush country, miles from any other humans. We decided to walk to the river, build a raft and float to Whitecourt. We reckoned without the muskeg. It was so bad that we nearly sank out of sight. We tried several different routes to the river, but not knowing the country we were finally forced to abandon our attempts.

"Food was our chief worry. I was going to put some grub aboard the plane when we left Grande Prairie, but Pete thought it was silly because we would be home in a few hours with everything going all right.

"But I had insisted on putting a slab of bacon on the plane. So that's all we had to eat. We stayed near the plane for four or five days and nights, figuring out the best thing to do. We were lucky enough to locate an old

May's plane at Grande Prairie in 1920 during his barnstorming days when the landing field was a river bar or pasture as shown in the photo.

cabin belonging to a forest ranger, so we had shelter there and a place to sleep. But were we ever hungry!

"Although the bacon wasn't very tasty it got us out of our jam. We looked the plane engine over and decided on trying something really novel. We rolled several pieces of bacon rind around the burned-out hose connection, and then wrapped all the friction tape we had over it. We filled the radiator with water and started the motor. Water still leaked out from around our makeshift repair, but it held fairly well.

"We got the old kite in the air all right and made for Whitecourt. It was soon apparent I would have to land again as we lost water fast and the motor was starting to heat again. So I picked another field beyond Whitecourt and landed.

"Here I decided to send Pete the rest of the way to town by train, so he headed for the railway station. I now had another problem. I needed more gasoline. The fuel problem was finally solved by using naptha lighting fluid I was able to get from a farmer. I wasn't at all sure how it would work, but the motor started up all right and I got back safely to Edmonton."

During his early barnstorming days May flew for Fred McCall, a fighter pilot from Calgary who in 1918 shot down thirty-seven German planes in six months to become one of the world's leading air aces. In France, May had probably saved McCall's life by shooting down a German plane which was on McCall's tail. The two became friends and in 1919 were barnstorming. On one of his flights that summer McCall experienced near disaster.

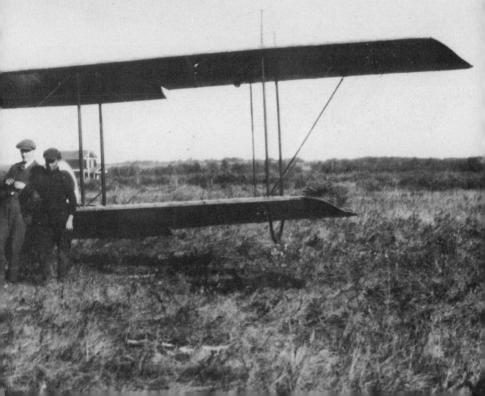

In his excellent book, *Canada's Flying Heritage,* pioneer aviator Frank H. Ellis describes what happened: "During the 1919 Calgary Exhibition, McCall was taking off from the infield on July 5, with two young sons of the exhibition manager as passengers. A few seconds after they were airborne, the engine cut out. McCall had to choose between landing in the middle of a track where an automobile race was in progress, or going down into a crowded midway. He chose the latter. With fine judgement he stalled the machine so that it dropped on the very centre of a merry-go-round, which was going full blast! No injury was suffered by pilot, passengers, or public; the roundabout withstood the impact, but the plane sustained considerable damage."

McCall resourcefully exhibited the plane at Edmonton the following week, charging 25 cents admission and selling pieces as souvenirs. He continued barnstorming until 1921 when, as he said, "We went broke, like most aviation pioneers."

In the meantime, May Airlines had been reorganized to include pilot George W. Gorman and become May-Gorman Airlines Limited. But 1922 brought disaster when Court May was killed in a non-flying accident. The tragedy profoundly affected Wop since he and his brother had been very close. Next year he sold his interest in the airline and worked for the rest of the year as a mechanic.

May spent the summer and autumn of 1924 barnstorming, then in November he married and went to Dayton, Ohio, to work for the National Cash Register Company. But he preferred Western Canada and returned to Edmonton in 1926, although still employed by NCR.

Flying remained his primary interest, however, and when a flying club was formed in Edmonton in 1927 he became its first president. Then in 1928 he received leave of absence from NCR to become a flying instructor. Thereafter he was to remain associated with flying for the rest of his life and that winter undertake a mercy flight which made him famous throughout North America.

The story began in 1928 when diphtheria broke out in the community of Little Red River some 80 km (50 miles) from Fort Vermilion in Northern Alberta. At Fort Vermilion, Dr. Harold Hamman, fearing for the lives of Little Red River's 150 residents and some 550 in his own community, sent an urgent request to the Alberta Board of Health for serum. A problem was that the only way to the outside world was by a nearly 480-km (300-mile) trek down the frozen Peace River by dog team. Two experienced dog mushers left Little Red River on December 18. So difficult was the journey that they were two weeks fighting their way to the community of Peace River which had railway and telegraph facilities.

Dr. M.R. Bow, Alberta's Deputy Minister of the Department of Health, finally received news of the outbreak on December 31. Two weeks had passed since Dr. Hamman had sent his urgent request for serum, and at the time the Hudson's Bay factor had already died and others were afflicted. Without the serum many of them would undoubtedly also die — if they hadn't already. There were only two ways for Dr. Bow to get the medication to the stricken communities—by train and dog team which could take up to three weeks, or by air. The only plane available, however, was a small Avro Avian owned by May and his partner, Vic Horner. It had two open cockpits, a 75-horsepower engine and wheels instead of skis, hardly the craft to challenge King Winter. But so desperate was the need for the serum that Dr. Bow contacted May.

Despite having to fly some 800 km (500 miles) over a winter wilderness in a plane totally unsuited to such conditions, May agreed. On January 2, 1929, the 9 kilograms (20 pounds) of serum were delivered to the airport by Dr. Bow, accompanied by Edmonton mayor A. Bury. May climbed into the rear cockpit, Vic Horner into the forward one. The serum was loaded aboard with a charcoal heater to keep it from freezing in the near 40 degree below zero temperature. At 12.45 p.m. the two took off from the frigid field.

Strong headwinds and blizzard-like conditions buffeted the tiny plane, cutting its speed well below its rated 100 miles an hour. After three hours they were forced to land at the hamlet of McLennan Junction about 80 km (50 miles) from Peace River. Authorities in Edmonton had fortunately envisioned the difficulties and telegraphed ahead to have a landing strip prepared. Residents cleared one on Round Lake and the plane landed safely. The following morning May and Horner were up before daybreak to clear ice and snow from the plane and try to start the engine. They had to drain the oil and warm it on a primus, then heat the engine with a blowtorch before it started. Once airborne they again encountered headwinds and were nearly an hour reaching Peace River Crossing.

They landed on the ice, fueled, then headed northward for Fort Vermilion. Because of its heavy fuel load, the plane refused to climb and May had to fly under the railway bridge which spanned the Peace River. They safely completed their journey over the snow-covered wilderness, arriving so numbed by cold and winds which created a chill factor equivalent to 110 degrees below zero that they had to be lifted from their cockpits. In addition their faces were frostbitten and covered with frozen blood from cuts caused by wind-driven snow particles. But their mercy mission was successful. A dog team was waiting to rush the serum to Little Red River and the only death was that of the HBC factor.

The two men returned to Peace River on January 5, once more so cold they had to be lifted from the aircraft, and so low on fuel that only one gallon remained. The following day they arrived at Edmonton in a blizzard, with May's fingers frozen to the controls. Despite the cold they received a rousing welcome from a crowd of several thousand, and cameramen from Fox-Movietone News informed all of North America of their exploit.

A month after the mercy flight, May, Horner and Cy Becker formed Commercial Airways, their sole asset the tiny plane in which May and Horner had made their dramatic flight. It was obvious to the three that a larger plane was needed. They somehow found the resources to purchase a Lockheed-Vega which had the luxury of a closed-in cabin. May and Horner

Part of the welcoming crowd at Edmonton when Horner, center in leather coat, and May, right in helmet, returned from their mercy flight.
At left Dr. Bow hands the diphtheria serum to May at the start of their 1929 flight which made them known throughout North America.

Unloading mail at Fort McMurray from the Bellanca on the inaugural flight of what was then the world's longest air mail route. The photo below shows May, center, during the Second World War with personnel of No. 2 Air Observer School at Edmonton.

arrived in Edmonton with it on February 10 and among its first flights was another mercy trip with diphtheria serum. In all, May flew six mercy missions in 1929 and made the first non-stop flight from Edmonton to Winnipeg, covering the 1,300 km (800 miles) in seven hours. In December alone he flew nearly 8,000 km (5,000 miles) between Fort McMurray and Aklavik on the Arctic Ocean, pioneering a new era for the north.

By then Commercial Airways had become associated with Rutledge Air Service to inaugurate a government sponsored air mail service from Edmonton to Aklavik. The 2,700-km (1,676-mile) route would be the world's longest and most northerly, over a wilderness covered with snow six months or more a year and mid-winter nights that lasted twenty hours and longer. May was given the responsibility of supervising the operation north of Fort McMurray to Aklavik. Among problems faced by pilots were the lack of airstrips, fuel depots and service facilities. Nevertheless, on December 10 the service was inaugurated with 120,000 letters from philatelists among several tons of mail.

On December 26, May landed at Aklavik in his red Bellanca, the "Lady Edmonton," with the first mail. The trip had taken sixteen days but the return took only four. The reason was given by Frederick B. Watt, a reporter for the *Edmonton Journal* who accompanied May on the inaugural flight. In the June 1930 issue of *Canadian Aviation* Watt wrote:

"The lengthy and arduous outward trip was attributable to a number of reasons. The bulk of the cargo was the chief of these. It was necessary to ferry the entire shipment ahead from post to post, with the result that when the two ships finally reached Aklavik they had each flown nearly 5,000 miles in covering the 1,676-mile route for the air mail.

"It was a case of flying into darkness as well. From Fort Simpson north the hours of daylight dwindled with breath-taking rapidity. Beyond Good Hope there was no sun at all, nor would there be for a matter of two weeks. The perpetual Arctic twilight, added to the perils of unknown landings, had cut the flying days decidedly short . . . ."

Watt's account also graphically describes the problems of servicing the aircraft in the intense cold and without shelter:

". . . It was 60° below zero F. at Fort Good Hope when we staged our Stag Christmas dinner in the Hudson's Bay Post. It was 54° below zero F. when we took off the next morning and crossed the Arctic Circle into territory never before seen from the air in winter. The actual flying wasn't so bad, but the business of preparing the ships for the night and the heating of engines in the morning contained few elements of humour. Frost-bitten hands and faces became too common to attract any attention. On two occasions Tim Sims and C. Van der Linden, guardian of the motors, worked until after midnight in 45° below zero F. temperatures to ensure dawn take-offs. One of these occasions was Christmas Eve and both of them occurred on the naked face of the Mackenzie with no hangar facilities and only the light of an electric torch to work by."

Despite the awesome obstacles, mail which had taken two months and longer to deliver by dog team now arrived in three or four days. For his achievement May was awarded the McKee Trophy as Canada's outstanding airman of 1929. Other awards were to come.

In 1929 May and his wife moved to Fort McMurray so that he could better supervise the formidable mail run and other activities of the fledgling airline. "My husband was often gone days and weeks at a time," Mrs. May recalled. "I learned to expect him when I saw him. I never used to be too worried about him."

In the following years, May flew many more mercy missions, pioneered new routes, and during the search for the Mad Trapper saved the wounded Hersey's life by flying him to Aklavik. International recognition of his contribution to northern flying came in 1935 when he was awarded the prestigious Order of the British Empire for "numerous mercy flights to outlying points in northwestern Canada."

But after nearly twenty years in the cockpit May was now increasingly tied to a desk. In March 1936 he became Superintendent of the Mackenzie River District for Canadian Airways which had absorbed Commercial Airways. A year later, as a result of an accident some years previously when he worked for National Cash Register, one of May's eyes was removed. His active flying days were over.

After the Second World War broke out May became deeply involved in the Commonwealth Air Training Program which trained tens of thousands of Allied airmen from all over the world. By now Canadian Airways had become part of Canadian Pacific Airlines which was operating several schools under the Air Training Program. May was appointed District Supervisor of Western Schools and then General Manager of all CPA's Air Observer Schools in Western Canada.

Despite this formidable responsibility, he found time to implement an idea that he felt would save the lives of pilots and crews who crashed in the wilderness. It was a first aid parachute team to drop into remote sites and provide assistance to survivors. For this service he was presented with the Medal of Freedom, Bronze Palm, by the United States.

The award noted, in part: "He conceived the idea of aerial rescue crews for rescue of fliers in the bush area, and after developing a trained parachute squad he furnished a rescue service indiscriminately to Americans and Canadians, thus saving the lives of many of our fliers. In so doing, he fulfilled the highest traditions of the Dominion of Canada."

After the war he continued with CPA in executive positions which included Director of Development. Unfortunately for Canadian aviation, on June 21, 1952, while vacationing with his family in Utah, May died of a heart attack. He was 57.

The *Calgary Albertan* probably best summarized his outstanding life of service when it noted: "The story of Capt. Wilfred Reid (Wop) May . . . is a parallel to the history of aviation in Canada."

His final awards came in 1973 when he was named a member of Canada's Aviation Hall of Fame, and in 1978 when the Historic Sites and Monuments Board of Canada unveiled a plaque in his honor at Edmonton's Municipal Airport. Sixty years before he had helped establish the airport, even though the public then showed little faith in the future of air transport. But May didn't share their views. To him air travel was not for the future, it was for the present. The subsequent course of aviation has proved the validity of his vision.

History from Heritage House

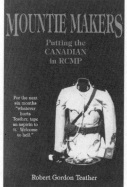

ISBN 1-894384-69-5
192 pp $16.95

ISBN 1-894811-41-4
160 pp $14.95

ISBN 1-895811-92-9
360 pp $27.95

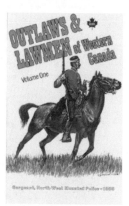

ISBN 1-894384-39-3
224 pp $18.95

ISBN 1-894384-70-9
192 pp $16.95

ISBN 1-895811-79-1
128 pp $10.95

Heritage House books are available
from local booksellers throughout western Canada.

Contact Heritage House Publishing Company Ltd. at
#108 - 17665 66A Avenue, Surrey, BC Canada V3S 2A7
Phone 604-574-7067 or 1-800-665-3302
Fax 604-574-9942 or 1-800-566-3336
greatbooks@heritagehouse.ca   www.heritagehouse.ca

Biographies from Heritage House

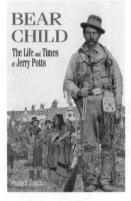

ISBN 1-894384-63-6
192 pp $17.95

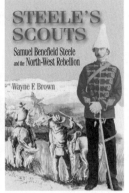

ISBN 1-894811-14-8
192 pp $16.95

ISBN 1-895811-43-1
224 pp $18.95

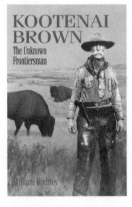

ISBN 1-894384-45-8
256 pp $18.95

ISBN 1-895811-63-5
240 pp $17.95

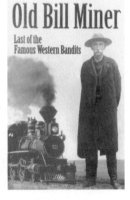

ISBN 1-894384-04-4
96 pp $9.95

www.heritagehouse.ca